MAKING A DIFFERENCE

How Being Your Best Self Can
*Influence, Inspire, and **Impel** Change*

YVETTE E. PEARSON

The
P EER
Group

Making a Difference
Copyright © 2022 Yvette E. Pearson

Printed in the United States of America

Requests for information should be addressed to:
The PEER Group, PO Box 56, McKinney, Texas 75070 | peergroupconsulting.com

ISBN (paperback): 979-8-9875487-0-7
ISBN (ebook): 979-8-9875487-1-4
ISBN (audio book): 979-8-9875487-2-1

Cover and interior design by KUHN Design Group | kuhndesigngroup.com
Edited by Helen Kalmans and Jacqueline Prince

To Geraldine E. Jackson, my greatest influence and champion; Amber Deanne, my "why"; and Travis Pearson, the best "Butta" in the world.

In loving memory of Eunice H. Jackson (ICUN Me), Travy Jackson, Paul Pearson, Terry Jackson, Sr., and Donald Jackson.

CONTENTS

PREFACE

"We can change the world and make it a better place. It is in our hands to make a difference."

NELSON MANDELA

If you're like me (and millions of other folks), you turn on the news multiple times per day curious about what has happened in the world since the last time you checked. After the first fifteen minutes, you're sorry you asked. Yet you still watch, you still listen; heartbroken by the pain, divisiveness, and evil that are so prevalent in the world and the resultant impacts on the local community, state, nation, and the global society.

Thankfully, it's not all gloom and doom. Later in the broadcast are the "feel good" stories, which I wish could come first, or at least bracket the bad ones so we could begin and end on positive notes. The stories about courage in the face of adversity, new records being set by athletes, awards being presented to performing artists, new book releases. Then there are the real heart-tuggers by journalists such as Steve Hartman and

David Begnaud that celebrate all the good there is in the world; stories that remind us of attributes such as kindness, gratitude, and selflessness.

One thing these stories have in common is that they all leave me with the thought, "What can I do to make things better?" I ponder how I can "show up" to help others mitigate the challenges they face by giving my gifts of time, influence, and resources to make a difference.

This book compiles lessons I've learned and strategies I've employed to live an authentic life, embracing who I am and using my background, identities, skills, and abilities to make a difference within my relatively small spheres of influence in this enormous world. It combines stories from my personal and professional life describing how I strive to avoid boxes so I'm not constrained by the norms and ideals of others; how I've learned to be comfortable but not content so I can leverage being the "first" and the "only" to help others thrive; how I found and began to effectively use my voice, including times I've missed the mark; how I navigate anger and use it strategically to impel change; and how I strive to leave things better than I found them in every area of my life, relying on "good home training" passed down through my elders to treat others well.

As you navigate this book, you'll encounter stories—some full of joy and inspiration and others that describe stress and pain. I contextualize some of the stories within constructs such as race, gender, and disability (as appropriate) so my positionality is clear and to illuminate the all-too-often disparate outcomes based on those factors, especially when they intersect. I share these stories with the hope you find them relatable and that they convey lessons that are transferable, if not directly applicable, to situations you've encountered.

If you identify with similar lived experiences, especially the difficult ones thinking, "That's happened to me" or "I'm going through that right now," I want you to know that you are not alone. And if you've shared victories similar to those you read here, I want to celebrate with you. If your lived experience shows up in a different way, as one who has created hurdles or barriers for others, thinking, "I've done (or said) things like that before," I hope you will reflect and change. And if you have been a bystander who has observed some of the things I describe—good or bad—thinking, "I've seen (or heard) things like that before," it is my desire that you will find the encouragement and motivation to get involved.

In all cases, my greatest wish is that through this book, you are inspired to be the best version of yourself and that your ability to influence, inspire, and impel change is strengthened so you are MAKING A DIFFERENCE—a positive difference—in the ways only you can.

1

INTRODUCTION

"None of us alone can save the nation or world.
But each of us can make a positive difference
if we commit ourselves to do so."

DR. CORNEL WEST

've done a lot of self-reflection to figure out why I gravitate toward certain opportunities and not others. It's something I've recognized in my professional life, my spiritual life, and in my personal life, and it shows up in both my relationships and my work. During a moment of reflection, I stumbled upon a memory.

When I was a child, my cousins and I were extremely close, so much so that we were often mistaken for siblings. We spent a great deal of time at each other's homes and we helped with chores. I remember being at one of my aunts' homes and having her ask my cousin and me to do some chore. Whether it was to wash dishes, clean the bathroom, or vacuum the floors—I don't remember. What I do recall is my mother noting that I was more enthusiastic (or maybe we'll say I responded more quickly) when it came to doing chores at my aunt's house than at our own.

I never realized it as a child, but in that moment of reflection as an adult, I remembered always being able to see the impact of what I'd done at my aunt's home. You see, my mom always kept our home pristine (except my room and my brother's, of course), so much so that you could almost eat off the floors (not that I would EVER do that; I'm too much of a germaphobe—even before COVID). When I did chores at home, it felt like I was doing things just because it was Saturday; Saturday mornings were set aside for chores in our house. My aunt's home, though it was clean, was a bit more "lived in." And so, when I did chores there, I could physically see the difference my work made. In that moment of reflection, I realized MAKING A DIFFERENCE was my motivation for everything.

SOW GOOD SEEDS

There are 7.8 billion people on Earth. While we were all created equal, we were also all created differently. My brother, Travis, and I talk often about how we are the products of the same parents, raised in the same household, and yet we are completely different from each other. No two people are identical; even "identical" twins have differences between them. This means that each of us brings something different to the world; there is something unique that is planted within each of us, much like a seed, that the world needs. It is our job as individuals to go through the journey of discovery to identify what that seed is, fertilize it and nurture it so that it grows and produces fruit for the benefit of others. Will the fruit from everyone's seeds be seen on the world stage? Probably not. Does that diminish the importance of the impacts of those fruit? Absolutely not! The seeds we sow, no matter how seemingly small, can make a world of difference in one person's life—good or bad. If each of us does our part to sow seeds of positivity, we can change the world—for good.

WORDS THAT HURT, WORDS THAT HEAL

Our words have power, as do our actions. We can say one negative thing or take one negative action and it can dampen someone's spirit and diminish their motivation, causing irreparable damage. When I graduated from high school, I had multiple universities that were trying to recruit me for their music programs. I played trombone and had been in All-Parish Bands and All-Parish Orchestras throughout my middle school and high school years (Louisiana's parishes are similar to counties in other states). During my last year in high school, I was in Louisiana's All State Jazz Ensemble. My band directors at Baton Rouge Magnet High School—Lee Fortier and John Gerbrecht—were renowned musicians. My bandmates included artists such as bassist Roland Guerin (Baton Rouge Magnet High School) and percussionist Brian Blade (All State Jazz Ensemble), though I'm far, far from being on par with them.

When I decided to attend Southern University instead of one of the universities that actively recruited me, Mr. Fortier told me, "If you go to Southern, you've gotta play with 'Bat'," referring to legendary jazz musician and composer,

Alvin Batiste. When I went to the university for my audition, Mr. Batiste was out of the country. Consequently, I ended up auditioning for another band director, a legend in his own right, who was equally renowned for his phenomenal work with bands (not jazz bands) and, at that time, for discrimination against women in his bands. For my audition with him, I masterfully played the same pieces I'd played for the All-State Jazz Ensemble, and his response was essentially, "And? Is that all you've got?" He made it clear that he heard nothing special in my playing. I packed my trombone, went home, and didn't open my case again until more than 13 years later.

By that time, I'd completed all three of my degrees and had been teaching at Southern in the College of Engineering for about six years. One of my students, who was a sax player, visited my home, where my (then) husband and I had an awesome rehearsal studio. He played keys and I mostly sang. We worked in music ministry and had a band together. Knowing this student was a musician, I invited him into the studio where he saw two trombone cases in the corner collecting dust.

He asked, "Hey Doc, who plays trombone?" I told him I did, in a former life. He encouraged me to pick it up again and invited me to go to his jazz improv class, which was taught by none other than Mr. Bat! Nervously, I took a late lunch one day and showed up a few minutes early for Mr. Bat's 1:00 class so I could introduce myself. I remember being in absolute awe when I met him! I mentioned that the student had invited me and asked if it was okay for me to sit in and learn. His response was, "The next time you want to learn something, bring your instrument." I attended his class—with my trombone—for most of the rest of that semester. I played gigs with the band, including the New Orleans Jazz Festival, during which he featured me on two songs. Fast forward more than a decade, I released an EP with my brother in 2017 under our stage name, "TraVet." It includes an instrumental piece, "Inspired," which is the theme song for my podcast, Engineering Change. I composed that song and am performing both the trombone and piano parts on it.

I can't help thinking—even now—about how much time, how many opportunities, and how much growth I lost because of one person's negative words. And oh my, how quickly things turned around with one person's words of encouragement and motivation. Just like we can say one negative word that destroys someone, we can say or do one thing that inspires, motivates, or creates an opportunity for one person, thereby sowing seeds of positivity into that person's life. Those seeds, when nurtured, will produce fruit that can impact countless others—people neither we nor the person whom we inspired may never know.

I hope that as you read this book, you are inspired to be uniquely and unapologetically you and that you will value differences—yours and others'—and leverage those differences to influence, inspire, and ultimately effect positive change, MAKING A DIFFERENCE—a positive difference—in someone's life, and hence, in the world.

2

AVOID BOXES

"People have so many hang-ups about how other people live their lives. People always want to keep you in a little box, or they need to label you and fix you in time and location. Although I did not recognize it at the time, I learned very early in life to avoid boxes."

ALICE WALKER

We've all been encouraged to "think outside the box." A box is a container that, by definition, serves the purpose of holding something. It's confining. It contains things within set boundaries. The concept of "thinking outside the box" challenges us to go beyond what is expected, typical, or conventional; to pursue ideas and pathways that are unconventional, atypical, and unexpected; to push beyond and go outside of the boundaries. But the box is still there. Its mere presence reminds us that there are certain conventions, norms, and expectations that others have established as boundaries within which we are expected to operate. I don't put myself in boxes and I don't take kindly to people trying to put me in boxes. I avoid boxes altogether.

AGAINST THE ODDS

If I lived according to what was "typical" or expected based on my background, I would not be where I am today. Being born a Black disabled woman who spent much of my child-hood in a small, rural community in southeast Louisiana, and whose parents divorced when I was in elementary school, sta-tistics didn't predict great outcomes for me. They didn't scream "future engineer!" Or "future vice president at a major univer-sity!" Or "future entrepreneur!" And certainly not all three. Yet here I am, leading a successful company that employs staff in six states (and counting) and nearly 30 years into a highly successful career in higher education, the vast major-ity of which has been in engineering.

I say this not to boast about myself, but in recognition that I did not—and could not—do these things by navigating life within pre-defined boundaries, nor could I do them on my own. My success and my ability to defy norms and expec-tations are rooted first and foremost in God. I believe God orders my steps, and because He "knit me together in my mother's womb" (Psalm 139:13), He crafted pathways and possibilities for me that others may not be able to conceive. If others can't understand my journey, why would I give them the control to navigate it? Why would I listen when they try to define what is or is not possible for me? Don't get me wrong, I value wise counsel; but there's a difference between receiving wise counsel and being confined by bound-aries others establish without cause.

Second is my mother, who amongst so many other things she has done, convinced me to major in engineering. She saw potential in me that I didn't see in myself. I asked her what it was that made her suggest that path for me and she said that she and my stepfather discussed it. And then she said something powerful: "I didn't want you to be in a box." You see, I was planning to major in music and foreign languages, and though I excelled in those areas, she saw narrow pathways of possibilities for my future had I pursued those majors. She was convinced, despite my lackluster high school performance, that I had the aptitude to succeed in any major I chose—music, foreign languages, engineering, computer science, or medicine (though I was too squeamish to be a doctor).

One thing I love about her pushing me to pursue engineering was that she did it by making a recommendation, not by exerting her authority and making a demand. In fact, she made it clear that I was free to shift gears if I decided engineering was not right for me. Even though I was her dependent, she did not try to put me in a box.

I've also learned to persevere. The ability to persevere has come from the circles of support God has built around me throughout my life. I have always been surrounded by people who believe in me, nurture me, and support me. My grandmother, Eunice, told me many times to get all the education I could get so I wouldn't have to depend on a man—or anyone else—to take care of me. Born in 1918, she could only dream of the opportunities I have as options because of her sacrifices and those of my other elders and ancestors. When I went to Southern, I found mentors such as Professor Huey

K. Lawson and Professor Edgar Blevins who were invested in my success, so much so that they would not allow me to give up during times I wanted to walk away from engineering. My aunts and uncles were second sets of parents who shared their wisdom, discipline, resources, and their stories with me. They prayed for me and reinforced the spiritual foundations my mother and my grandmother set—and they still do. They have taught me how to challenge convention and win; how to work within systems to ultimately change them. All these things have worked together to keep me far removed from the confinement of boxes for as long as I can remember.

CHALLENGING CONVENTION

I remember when I was an undergraduate engineering student interviewing for a summer internship (way back in the 1900s as my daughter would say). Our career services office had a lot of wonderful resources to help us prepare for interviews—resume reviews, mock interviews, career fairs—the works. They also seemed to focus quite a bit on dress code—especially for women. Our dress code guidance was based on convention and societal norms at the time, which dictated that women should not wear pants or pantsuits to interviews (I am dating myself). We were told that we should wear suits with skirts or business-appropriate dresses. A box. I encountered the same thing at church. Many churches forbade women to wear pants. Some forbade pants in the sanctuary; others forbade pants for women altogether. And while the churches I attended didn't have it as a written rule, it was pretty much an unspoken rule that women wore dresses or skirts to church.

I've always hated dresses. When I was a kid, I was more likely to shop in a western store with my dad and wear jeans with boots or tube socks and sneakers than I was to wear dresses or skirts. Even now, my staff knows I don't like dresses. If they see me in the office wearing a dress or a skirt, they know that I have not done laundry and I'm at the bottom of the barrel with my wardrobe. I hate being put in a box labeled "women and girls should wear dresses."

A friend asked me if I would feel so strongly against wearing skirts and dresses if it was not an institutionalized expectation, and my answer was, "I don't know." As I often do when I'm processing things and trying to understand myself, I asked my mom where she thought my dislike for all things "girly" originated. She pointed out that my dad, who was known as the "Black Cowboy," wanted me to be strongly identified with him from an early age. Being a "daddy's girl," I had no problem with that. I knew that's where my preference for western wear, jeans, sneakers, and the like began. In talking through this with my mother, I realized that somewhere along the way, it was no longer just about preference. I came to despise being expected to wear certain things—or not to wear certain things—when it was something folks tried to force on me with no good reason rather than it being a choice I was able to make for myself.

Another thing I remember from the career services office's guidance was that we shouldn't wear red to an interview because red is an "aggressive" color. Another box. Outside of school, I was taught that red represented power, leadership, and authority. Behzad Mohebbi's research in organizational leadership and branding identifies the color red with a total of 21 attributes (Mohebbi, 2014). Over half of them are positive and include things like love, passion, strength, energy, power, and leadership. Only a small fraction of them is negative: danger, war, anger, etc.; and some are neutral: masculinity, revolution, etc. Who gets to decide what a color means at a given time or in a particular situation? Why is it that we were told that wearing red would represent one of a handful of negative characteristics rather than one or more of numerous positive ones?

I showed up for my interview. It was with Exxon (before it became ExxonMobil). And what did I wear? A red blazer, a white blouse, and navy slacks—the company colors. I was looking the part! And guess what? I got the job. I guess the interviewer didn't care too much about "convention" when it came to me—a woman—wearing pants and my (my mother's) red blazer.

Much later in life, when I was married, the pastor of our church pulled a few couples together to discuss our being appointed as deacons. My (then) husband and I attended a meeting where they discussed the expectations. I'll be honest. The only thing I recall from that meeting was someone saying that I could no longer wear pants to church. Apparently, there was an anointing on my life that drew them to extend this invitation to me—pants and all. Now suddenly, pants were forbidden. We politely declined (I'm sure there were other reasons that contributed to that decision, but this is what I can remember).

Sometimes it takes someone stepping, not just thinking, outside of the box—or better yet, avoiding the box altogether—to help people see things differently and promote a paradigm shift that disrupts the status quo. It's okay if that someone is you. Of course, now, seeing women in pantsuits has become mainstreamed in not only churches but also in business and politics. Two words: Hillary Clinton.

On the surface, you might question why I led with "women in pants" as a box. This is, indeed, something that appears simplistic and relatively innocuous; however, I have found over time that things progress little by little until they get to a point of no return. If we allow ourselves to be put in boxes with little things, we will accept being in boxes—being constrained—as our norm.

Mississippi Mass Choir released a song several years ago about caged birds. A man bought a set of caged birds. He opened the cage door to release them, and they would not fly away. They had the opportunity to be free but remained confined. The constraints placed on them by the cage, which in this case was a physical constraint, bound them not only physically, but also mentally. Their confinement had, in essence, trained them that they were not supposed to be free. In the same way, if we're not careful, we can let constraints, conventions, and societal norms confine us such that we think we are not supposed to have certain things, achieve successes that others achieve, or be in certain positions.

The best way to avoid this is to avoid boxes. As far as it is within your power, don't confine yourself to a box, and don't let others confine you to boxes or constrain you within their human perceptions or misconceptions of limitations.

Here are three of the things I have found helpful that you might consider putting into practice. First, ask and answer "why" questions. Why am I doing this? Why do I want to do this? Why are we doing things this way? If the answers are along the lines of "other folks are doing it" or "this is the way it's always been done," then you're likely in—or headed toward—a box.

The next questions to be asked and answered should be "what" questions. What different outcomes am I trying to achieve? What can I do differently to produce those outcomes? When we understand "why" and "what," we can then begin to work on the "how." Often our efforts fail because we dive in without a plan. When we take the time to understand why we are where we are in addition to what we are trying to do, we can be more effective in developing intentional plans that have higher likelihoods of success and are less constrained by limitations others face.

Second, develop yourself strategically and unconventionally. Work on your strengths. Just because we have gifts and talents in certain areas does not mean they do not need to be honed. And there's nothing that requires us to spend countless amounts of time and energy working on our weaknesses. We all have areas of weakness—things we can't do, things we don't know. And that's okay. That's one of the reasons we need people; other people are strong in areas where we are weak. I recall a major "aha" moment when I read Dean Graziosi's book, *Millionaire Success Habits* a few years ago. He stated:

> *By focusing on your weaknesses… you end up feeling inferior subconsciously. Just as troubling, this focus encourages you to ignore your exceptional capabilities and strengths (Graziosi, 2019).*

Feelings of inferiority lead to boxes. To avoid boxes, we need to build—and utilize—our unique abilities, and that involves investing time and resources into further developing the strengths that are needed to accomplish our plans.

Finally, embed people in your inner circle who believe in you and who will challenge you. One of the biggest hindrances in many of our lives is that we limit ourselves based on other people's expectations. We need people in our innermost circles who will speak the truth to us, which is not always reality. Reality is limited to what we can see, and we cannot allow the unseen possibilities we are striving to attain to be hindered by limitations that exist in others' minds. We need people who will encourage and support us, even when they cannot see exactly what we envision for ourselves. And we need people who will bring our names up in rooms we may not yet be able to enter. The bottom line—we need people. Regardless of what folks say, no one is "self-made."

> Take a moment to reflect. What boxes have con-
> strained you? Who placed them there? How did
> you get into them? How can you get out of them?
> How might you avoid similar boxes going forward?

OVERCOMING LIMITATIONS

One of the quickest ways to motivate me to do something—if it's something I want to do—is for someone to tell me they don't think I can or should do it. I can trace this back to my childhood. I was born with cerebral palsy (CP). I have spastic hemiplegia, meaning CP causes my muscles to be constantly stiff, sometimes resulting in awkward, jerky movements; and it affects half my body (the right side). Although my mobility hasn't always been as limited as it is now (I require mobility aids such as walkers and crutches to get around the house and a wheelchair to get around most other places), I've always had limitations. My right arm and hand have a lot of spasticity, and I can't control it. I can't open my right hand. It stays in a fist, a tightly clenched fist. I can use my left hand to force it open, but when I let it go, it closes right back up. I have some control of my forefinger and thumb on my right hand, but very little. In recent years, I've also slowly lost the use of my right arm and am in near-constant pain.

My dad used to tell me stories about when I would go to physical therapy as a child. He mentioned to the therapist that I was showing interest in piano. We always had a piano in our house because my mom plays. My dad told me one of the therapists said something like, "Oh no! you can't let her try that. It's going to be a major catastrophic failure that will impact her for the rest of her life." Well, perhaps "major catastrophic failure" wasn't exactly what she said, but the notion was that my parents should not encourage me to try something like playing piano, which requires the full use of two hands. Or does it?

The therapist was trying to put me in a box when I was three or four years old, and I had no idea! I know now from the literature that one of the greatest factors that hinders success for students with disabilities is low expectations (Sanders, 2006; Butrymowicz and Mader, 2017; Pearson and Alexander, 2020). When the focus is on what people can't do rather than what they *can* do, it sends a message to them that can then manifest in low performance, regardless of what their actual aptitudes and abilities are. This is one example of how stereotype threat works.

> People can be adversely affected by negative ste-
> reotypes, so much so that they become inescapable,
> or what some refer to as "self-fulfilling prophecies."
> This is the phenomenon Dr. Claude Steele and
> Dr. Joshua Aronson defined as "stereotype threat"
> (Steele and Aronson, 1995).

I marveled when my dad told me the story about my physical therapist after I became an adult because I was clueless about that exchange. Thankfully, my parents didn't let my disability override my ability. They didn't put me in any boxes, nor did they allow anyone else to do so. Beyond that, they never made me feel as if I had any limitations; no one in my family did. Honestly, while I recognized that I had to do some things a bit differently from others, I don't recall seeing my disability as a limitation until much later.

I took piano lessons beginning at age five and continued through about fourth or fifth grade. I started playing trombone in sixth grade, which requires the use of my right hand and arm to slide to the seven positions. I played trombone throughout middle school and high school, received numerous honors (including All-Parish Bands, All-Parish Orchestras, All-State Jazz Ensemble), and picked it up again later in life. I resumed piano in high school as well under the tutelage of the late, great Drew Shaw. I never had a conversation with Mr. Shaw to ask for simpler or modified songs. He would assign sheet music for pieces by Chopin (Prelude in E Minor,

Opus 28, No. 4), Neidlinger and Powers (Birthday of a King), and other notable composers. I figured out how to play them although I was only able to fully use my left hand and was limited to using only the forefinger and thumb on my right hand.

I emphasize the limitations with my right hand because many people can probably conceptualize playing piano with limited left-hand use. The right hand is where a lot of the action happens—melodies, chords, arpeggios. I figured out how to compensate as much as I could with my left hand. I crossed my hands, playing treble with my left and bass with my right; I played two of three or more notes within chords with my thumb and forefinger; I extended the thumb on my left hand to play lower notes in the treble clef. Sometimes I would do all three at different points within the same song.

I remember going to a piano competition at LSU when I was in high school and as I started playing my piece, the judge pointed out that I was not using proper fingering. I had to stop playing and explain to him my disability. I eventually asked if he would just close his eyes and listen to me play the piece. And he did. I got a "Superior" rating and was on my way. My physical limitation did not impact my ability to execute that piece of music. Had the judge not watched me play from the beginning he would not have known I was any different from any other pianist.

Think about that for a moment. How much of what we see in terms of who can be "successful" in the music industry (as one example) is based on limitations set by someone's pre-defined "ideals," which are all boxes? If you don't get into the industry by a certain age, you might as well not try. If you are a woman and don't look a certain way or you are larger than a size six—hang it up. If you are disabled, forget it; if you have a physical disability, you might not even be able to get onto the stage, let alone experience "belonging" there.

Thank God for the folks who defy those boxes. Stevie Wonder, who is blind, has been *the* premier musician, singer, and songwriter for decades. One of my fondest memories is having a front row seat at his "Songs in the Key of Life" concert in Washington, DC in 2014 because he chose to reserve wheelchair accessible seating on the front row at regular ticket prices. I haven't attended any other concerts where that was done. This is only one small example of how Stevie Wonder's being "out the box" makes a difference, not only in music, but also in the world. Lizzo, another award-winning singer, songwriter, musician, and actress, has stood on the front lines to battle against folks who have tried to body shame her and other curvaceous women such as myself. She employs women of color of all body types to share the stage with her as musicians, singers, and dancers. At the age of 95, Angela Alvarez became the oldest person nominated for—and to win—a Grammy. In 2022, she tied with a 25-year-old and won best new artist at the Latin Grammys.

While these are huge success stories with honors that are hard-earned and well-deserved, they are the exceptions that are rare in the music industry. How many of us have given up on our dreams not because we were not good enough or didn't work hard enough, but because we knew we could not fit the boxes that define who gets to make it in a specific field or career and who doesn't? Boxes that are not based on skills and ability, but on surface-level attributes that are defined by a small subset of the population and exclude a large fraction of folks.

HURDLES AND BARRIERS

Except for being bullied when I was young because I was different, "disability" was not something I thought about every day. I thought about it when I experienced difficulties with some things; but, if there was something I wanted to do, my mindset was that I just had to figure out a way to do things a bit differently from other people. I think this is part of what taught me that we deal with whatever circumstances we are given in life and do our best to make the most of them.

Now don't get me wrong. I'm not promoting the mantra "adapt and overcome" here. Too often persons with disabilities, especially those with invisible disabilities, are told to "get over it" as if they can turn a switch on or off to control their difficulties—and that is WRONG. The same holds true for other boxes or constraints people face that are beyond their control. What I am saying is that we all face different circumstances and challenges in life that limit us in some way. If you haven't faced any, just keep living—you will.

Each of our challenges takes on different forms. Some are physical, some are mental, some are emotional, some are socioeconomic, relational, etc. Some are intrinsic and others are extrinsic. Some extrinsic challenges create or exacerbate intrinsic challenges. In all cases, we must strive to be our best selves—whatever that looks like—making the most out of every opportunity and circumstance. Also in all cases, when we are in the position to mitigate the challenges that others face because of systemic failures or other things beyond their control, it is our responsibility to do so.

I like to think of challenges and limitations in two broad categories: barriers and hurdles. Barriers block our movement; impede our progress. If I'm in my wheelchair and I encounter a four-inch curb with no ramp or curb cutout, it is a barrier to me. My progress in the direction of and my ability to get onto that curb are impeded. At that point, I have three choices: sit there and stare at the curb, ask for help, or change directions and find another path. The latter two options, in effect, turn a barrier into a hurdle. When we can change courses and turn barriers into hurdles—or remove them altogether, we must consider how we might not only do so for ourselves, but also for the benefit of others who follow.

I chose the curb cutout example because it's one that I've encountered frequently. At one of my previous institutions, I used campus buses to get to and from one of our research centers. The campus had two types of wheelchair accessible buses: large ones that had ramps that folded out of the main door next to the driver and rested on the curb, and small ones that had lifts on the back. The small ones were the ones that served the research center.

On one side of the center was a loading and unloading zone for bus passengers. The problem was that it did not have any curb cutouts, and therefore was not fully accessible (compliant is not always accessible). When I traveled to the center, the bus driver had to park the bus at the intersection (which did have a curb cut), get out, and operate the lift for me to enter or exit the bus. It was scary because cars were approaching the intersection from opposite directions and their drivers could not see each other. This arrangement was the epitome of "an accident waiting to happen." The only other option would have been for me to exit the rear of the small bus at the loading/unloading zone and roll down the street to the curb cut, which was just as unsafe.

One day, I had my phone in hand and grabbed a photo of one of these near accidents. I'd mentioned the accessibility problem to a facilities committee before, but nothing had been done. It's amazing how fast the problem was corrected when I shared the picture of the two cars that had unknowingly wandered into a game of "chicken." As a result, what had been a barrier and a major safety hazard—for not just me, but also for others whom I'll never know—was removed. Not only was a curb cut added at that bus stop; the committee proceeded to evaluate other stops across the campus and at university-owned apartments off campus to ensure they were both safe and accessible.

Unlike barriers that are designed to block our path, hurdles are obstacles that are designed to be overcome. If we think of this in terms of track and field, hurdles MUST be overcome for a runner to win the race. But doing so takes practice. Hurdlers learn to overcome hurdles by jumping hurdles. They train by first learning techniques to overcome smaller hurdles, which they apply to larger ones. In life, sometimes we end up training on the larger hurdles early on, so much so that when we're older, we can conquer anything.

Having to overcome limitations from a young age equipped me to overcome many other challenges as I've grown older. In contrast, sometimes people go through the early stages of life never having to overcome any hurdles; the hurdles were removed from their path, or their areas of privilege allowed them to go around them. This is detrimental when they face hurdles later because they've had no practice, and no training to help them overcome obstacles. In cases like this, or in situations when we're tired of running and jumping, hurdles can become barriers.

CHARTING YOUR OWN PATH

I mentioned earlier that I have been in higher education for nearly 30 years. Most career paths in academia have a typical, normative progression, either on the tenure track or a non-tenure track. Bear with me as I try to describe.

Some start with a postdoctoral appointment after completing the Ph.D., then move through the ranks of assistant, associate, and full professor, typically earning tenure simultaneously with the rank of associate professor. Afterward, if faculty are interested in administration, they might become department chairs, then deans, then provosts, or perhaps associate deans, then chairs, deans, and provosts.

Different universities have different categories of non-tenure track faculty. Some progress in rank as assistant, associate, and full teaching professors; some are lecturers, instructors, or professors of practice typically with no available progressions in faculty ranks. Non-tenure track faculty focus primarily on teaching, advising, and service; relatively few of them move into administration.

My career has followed a unique, circuitous path that has encompassed tenure-track, tenured, and non-tenure track faculty positions; administration and staff appointments; service as a federal program officer; and consulting—and it's still evolving. I'm still evolving. I started as a tenure track assistant professor in the Department of Civil Engineering at Southern University (my alma mater and one of the nation's Historically Black Colleges and Universities, or HBCUs) after earning a master's degree (something that is rare, especially today). After a few years, I went back to school and earned a Ph.D., and a few years after returning to work, became a tenured associate professor.

I left Southern to take a non-tenure track faculty position at the University of Texas at Arlington. I had colleagues at Southern who supported me, and others who questioned, and even ridiculed, me. The latter would say things like, "Why are you doing that? You're taking a step backward. You're going from an HBCU to a Predominantly White Institution (PWI). You're not going to have the respect of the students or your colleagues. You're just checking boxes for them."

Thankfully, UT Arlington was nothing like that. I was, indeed, taking a step backward in terms of title and tenure; however, that step back gave me momentum for steps forward and upward that I couldn't even begin to imagine at the time. I often equate this to the action of shooting a slingshot, or better yet, a bow and arrow (since my name means "archer"). To generate the energy needed to shoot the arrow forward, the archer has to pull back and then release. I feel this "pulling back" in my career enabled me to develop and release a tremendous amount of kinetic energy that has propelled me forward, and I have not looked back.

Again, I was in a non-tenure track position at UT Arlington (by choice), which does not require research or other grant funding. I won a Research Excellence Award from the College of Engineering during my second year. The funny thing was that I had no idea those awards existed. I remember signing for the check in absolute shock when one of the administrative assistants brought it to my office. I'd pursued funding from the National Science Foundation (NSF) to support students because it was my passion, not because of any job requirements, and certainly not in search of any award.

A few years later, I was appointed associate chair of the department, which again, was not so common for non-tenure track faculty. A couple of years later, NSF recruited me to serve as a program director. Program directors manage all aspects of the research programs for the agency—research priorities, program development, budgets, the review process, portfolio balance, etc. Again, I had (and took advantage of) this opportunity as a non-tenure track (i.e., a non-research) faculty member.

From there, I became an associate dean in the School of Engineering at Rice University (as a staff member with no faculty appointment) and I started a consulting firm, The Pearson Evaluation and Education Research Group (The PEER Group) shortly thereafter. These experiences, including all the successes and challenges that came with them, uniquely equipped me for my current appointment as a vice president at the University of Texas at Dallas. Because I've experienced academia in so many roles and from so many perspectives, I can bring that to the job to optimally serve our campus community.

The moral of the story is this. Don't let people put you in boxes defining what your career path—or any other path—should look like. Don't get me wrong; it's great to learn from the experiences of others—both good and bad experiences. I've always advised my students and protégés to find someone who's doing what they think they may want to do in the future, learn how they got to where they are, and learn what they would do differently if they could. I do this myself. These types of lessons learned can be of tremendous value as you're charting your course. However, in learning from others, you must be careful not to limit yourself based on their experiences. Everyone's path is unique. Everyone's circumstances are different. Chart your own course.

Start with *people*. Throughout his seminal book, *Good to Great*, Jim Collins repeats the phrase, "First who, then what" (Collins, 2001). He uses the metaphor of a bus when describing how leaders "drive" their companies.

> *The executives who ignited the transformations from good to great did not first figure out where to drive the bus and then get people to take it there. No, they first got the right people on the bus (and the wrong people off the bus) and then figured out where to drive it (Collins, 2001).*

This principle is transferable to many contexts. Build your circle of support. Who are the people who are not confined by boundaries and boxes? Who are the people you can go to completely unguarded to seek wise counsel in different areas—personal, professional, spiritual, financial? The people who can "speak the truth in love" and help you navigate the challenges that come with their counsel, when needed. These might be people you see every day, such as family members; or they might be mentors, advisors, or coaches you check in with a few times per year. And keep in mind, these people might change over time depending on where you are in your journey.

I had different mentors when I was married than I've had as a single person. My mentor network grew and evolved when I decided to pursue writing and speaking. When I started my business, I built relationships with people who have been successful in similar businesses for years. My spiritual mentors have changed as I've evolved and matured. Think about who you need in your inner circle, reach out to them—or ask for an introduction through a mutual connection—and use your time with them wisely. Always have questions. Learn from their journeys.

Always have a *plan* so you're not wandering aimlessly into your future; and be flexible enough to take detours along the way, if necessary. Unexpected, rewarding opportunities might be awaiting you. Think of "what if" scenarios that are possible ways things may go differently from what you expected.

When I'm consulting clients on evaluation as they are developing their project ideas, I ask them to consider unforeseen factors that might impact the project—both positively and negatively. To the extent possible, they can address those factors in their project plans. Then I define a strategy for capturing and providing feedback and recommendations on those factors as a part of our evaluation plan. You can't plan for everything but being thoughtful about "what ifs" can help you overcome challenges you encounter and recognize opportunities that can expand or deepen the impacts of your efforts.

Then *prepare*. In addition to preparing for "what ifs," you can further prepare by equipping yourself with every tool (i.e., skills and abilities) you can so that when unexpected opportunities arise, you'll be in a position to take advantage of them. Take an online class, read books, or listen to podcasts to learn more about your areas of interest and how things are changing in your field. Hone your skills, strategically building your strengths so you can apply them in a variety of contexts.

I attended proposal development workshops early in my career so I could learn how to be successful in obtaining grant funding for initiatives to support my students. Having that tool in my tool belt has led to many opportunities beyond my imagination. I had no idea that my successes in pursuing grant funding would lead to me becoming a program officer at the federal agency that has funded most of my work. And I never conceived that I would have a business with clients who pay me to help them develop proposals for funding to support their students, impacting lives I'll never touch individually.

Finally, ***persevere***. Don't give up just because things get hard. Sometimes things become difficult because they are designed as training hurdles; we need to overcome them so we can successfully overcome bigger hurdles that come later. At other times things become difficult because we've grown complacent, or things no longer fit the path intended for us. The difficulties we face in those situations can be the factors that motivate us to pursue change. Some of my major job transitions have happened at these junctures.

Sometimes things are difficult because of systemic barriers that are designed to break us down and make us fail. In these circumstances, we must shift from a mindset of persevering to self-preservation. I have counseled some of my protégés to leave their jobs because the environments were toxic and, in some cases, were beginning to harm their mental and physical health in addition to their professional well-being. I almost left academia at one point because of the toxicity I faced from colleagues and some administrators. Perseverance does not supersede self-care.

Now back to people. Phenomenal Grammy award-winning singer, songwriter, and musician Jonathan McReynolds has a song called "People." It starts:

> *They are the best and the worst You've created; loving and hating and opinionated. Loners in basements and those congregated—deliver me (McReynolds, 2020).*

While people can be some of our greatest supporters and champions, they can also be huge stumbling blocks. And sometimes the biggest and loudest naysayers are those who are closest to us. Don't let people deter you because what you're doing is different, or even strange to them. Your path is uniquely yours. And your unique path will give you experiences and insights that will help you as you're MAKING A DIFFERENCE in ways that no one except you can.

3

BE COMFORTABLE
BUT NOT CONTENT

"While I may be the first woman in this office, I will not be the last… Dream with ambition, lead with conviction and see yourselves in a way that others may not, simply because they've never seen it before."

VICE PRESIDENT KAMALA HARRIS

As a Black, disabled, woman engineer, I constantly find myself being the "only" or even the "first" in a lot of situations. I've learned to be comfortable with this, but not to be content with it. Comfort and contentment are two different things, in my opinion. When we're comfortable, we are relaxed; we're at ease. So being comfortable with being the "only" or the "first" means we're not uptight, intimidated, or stifled in our ability to perform because no one else in certain circles shares our identities. Contentment, on the other hand, is essentially satisfaction. I think of it as an extreme level of comfort. When we are content with something, we've gotten so comfortable with it that we're okay if it never changes. There are people within our schools, companies, governments, and communities who are content with the status quo. Sadly, there are people from minoritized and marginalized identities who are content being the "only" in their positions. Instead of being trailblazers who become gateways for others, they become gatekeepers, often hindering others from reaching their level of "success."

BEING COMFORTABLY DISCONTENT

Reflecting on my childhood again, I was never forced to conform to any stereotypes related to my race, gender, or disability. I found myself flying solo many times. That, I believe, gave me a firm foundation for managing what I would end up experiencing later in life—as a graduate student and as a professional who still is often the only Black person, the only woman, the only Black woman, the only person with a disability or the only Black disabled woman in the room.

Among the earliest things I rejected (though unknowingly at the time) were gender stereotypes. Did I mention that I've always hated to wear dresses? The truth is, I hated anything people associate with being "girly." I didn't like pink. I didn't like floral prints. I didn't like dolls. My mom still reminds me of a time she and my dad gave me a doll for Christmas. The story is that I took it outside and threw it across the fence to the neighbor's dog. That was the last doll they bought for me.

What did I like? Train sets, racetracks, Hot Wheels®, and trucks—good old Tonka® trucks. (They didn't make Tonkas out of plastic in my day; they made them out of metal that might have been coated with lead-based paint for all I know). In retrospect, it seems I was the only girl who did not like "girly" things. But who created that box? Who decided that "dolls are for girls" and "balls (and trucks and trains) are for boys"? Why was I considered a "tomboy?" Why couldn't I just be a girl who liked toy trains, race cars, trucks, and "cowboy" boots?

I started seeing the difference with my disability, race, and gender after I went to school. I was bullied because of my disability. I recall being in preschool and playing alone. When playtime came, the other kids always beat me to the Tinker Toys® (predecessors to Lego® for you youngsters) and no one would play with me. I hated that place. I dropped out of preschool.

When I went to kindergarten, I avoided recess altogether. I chose to stay inside and help my teacher or read instead. I'm sure I was the only kid who did not like or look forward to recess. I believe my teacher became concerned about my social development, so she worked with my parents to force me to go to the playground for recess. I remember going out one day, and a group of kids pinned me down on the ground. They called me "cripple," punched me in the stomach, and said things like, "Kindergarten baby, stick your head in gravy." Yes, I still remember it well. After that, I spent my recess periods reading. If I had to go outside, I sat next to the classroom door and read. I was reading books far above my grade level. My favorite that year was a mystery titled *The Ghost of Windy Hill*.

Throughout elementary school and much of middle school, I remember girls playing a lot of hand games like Miss Mary

Mack, Slide, and Rockin' Robin. They were afraid to play with me because they thought if they touched my hand, they would catch what I had and wouldn't be able to open their hands. Sadly, I remember telling people, "I'm not contagious" with hopes they'd let me play with them. I realized when I got older that their fear was based on a lack of awareness and a lack of knowledge (much like the unfounded fear and the lack of knowledge that contribute to the educational, workplace, and societal inequities today). Nevertheless, it was cruel and mean.

As a result of being rejected by the girls' playgroups, I began playing with the boys. I have a cousin, Terry; he and I grew up along with our cousin, Andrea, like brother and sisters. We are stair-stepped in age (I'm the baby of that bunch); peas in a pod. I would play basketball with Terry and his friends at his house, so the guys in the neighborhood came to know that I played basketball well. When I was in fourth grade, the guys started to invite me to play ball with them at recess. They didn't care that I was a girl. They just wanted to play with somebody who could hoop. I was the only girl on the court playing basketball at recess instead of doing whatever the other girls were doing.

Although I was isolated in a lot of situations before, this fourth-grade experience was the first time I recall recognizing that I was "the only" something. Since that time, I've been the only or the first in many more situations.

> I was the only girl trombone player in my middle school and high school bands.

I was the only Black student in the gifted and talented program at my first middle school.

I transferred middle schools and the new one had a "gifted side" and a "regular side." (How's that for inclusion)? On the "gifted side," I was one of only a few Black students in eighth grade.

I was the only girl in my high school jazz ensemble for my first two years.

Over time I grew to embrace being "the only." I grew to like it because it made me stand out; I tended to kind of shrink back from things because of my early childhood experiences. I grew to be content with it. I liked being the "only" and wasn't keen on having someone follow my footsteps, not realizing that was a detrimental mindset.

The good part of being comfortable with "onlyism" was that when faced with being "the only" later in life, I was able to not only survive it, but I was able to thrive.

When I started my faculty career at Southern University, I was the only woman professor in my department. I was also the only American-born faculty member in the department.

When I moved to the University of Texas at Arlington, I was one of only two women faculty and the only Black employee in my department (there were no other Black faculty or staff members). I was the only Black woman faculty member in the whole College of Engineering, and it was a large college.

When I got to Rice in 2016, I was the first Black associate dean at the university. I recall telling my mom that this made me both proud and sad at the same time. But I digress.

I discovered as an adult that while I'm comfortable being "the only," I'm not content with it. I don't want to be "the only." As a result, I have spent most of my career thinking of people like me—those who don't "fit the mold" of other people's images of an engineering student, an engineer, a faculty member, an administrator—and crafting programs and strategies to level the playing field so they can, hopefully, have a few less or perhaps a little lower hurdles to overcome than I did.

Don't get it twisted. Leveling the playing field does not equate to lowering standards or expectations, contrary to what some people believe. It's about removing systemic barriers—those inequities that are baked into the very fabric of engineering education and practice, higher education, and society more broadly—that inhibit equal and equitable opportunities for people from racially and ethnically minoritized identities, women, disabled people, persons from socioeconomically disadvantaged backgrounds, and multiple intersecting marginalized identities to succeed.

TOKENISM AND TWOKENISM

Years ago, I had a conversation with a university administrator who was part of a search committee that was formed to hire someone to help improve diversity and inclusion among faculty in their engineering and science programs. At some point in our conversation, he said something like this:

> *We have a Black faculty member; we have a few women. We have a couple of Hispanics… And I had to tell them that they were both Hispanic. I said, 'Did you know he was Hispanic? Did you know she was Hispanic?' They didn't even know! Oh, and Asians—we have enough of them so we're doing okay there. We need to do better with women, Blacks, and Hispanics.*

For institutions of higher education, professional societies, corporations, government agencies, or any organizational entity to see a change in the representation of people from minoritized and marginalized identities, they must immediately abandon this checklist approach. It does nothing for improving and sustaining diversity because the systems that create and perpetuate inequities for people from marginalized identities remain intact.

When organizations limit their diversity efforts to a checklist, it amounts to tokenism, "the practice of doing something (such as hiring a person who belongs to a minority group) only to prevent criticism and give the appearance that people are being treated fairly" (Encyclopedia Britannica, 2022). I believe one reason for the perpetuation of "onlyism" is the threat people from minoritized and/or marginalized identities sometimes experience when they reach certain levels of attainment or achievement.

There's a well-known saying that "perception is reality," so whether real or perceived, the threat is real to the person experiencing it. I believe this comes, in part, from tokenism. When people realize their organization only "allows" one woman or one Black person or one [fill in the marginalized identity] in a given position or at a given level, it creates an unhealthily competitive situation in which they feel they must "guard" their spot, resulting in people being gatekeepers who block access and progress rather than gateways who are willing to mentor others or help create opportunities and pathways for others to follow. Because God forbid, there would be 50 percent women in leadership positions or representation among the leaders that in any way reflected our diverse society (she said, with tongue firmly planted in cheek).

To keep up appearances, many organizations have appointed two people from marginalized identities, usually women (but not women of color), to leadership positions. This practice, recognized as "twokenism," has the same effect as tokenism.

Don't fall into the trap of expecting people from minoritized identities to carry the load on mentoring or service-oriented work. This "diversity tax" is a burden that creates further marginalization and inequity. An organization that is serious about diversity, equity, and inclusion (DEI) integrates it into policies and practices, which includes expectations and accountability for everyone to do their part. They also provide people with education and resources to do the work well.

GATEWAYS AND GATEKEEPERS

A few years ago, I had the great pleasure of watching the movie Hidden Figures with my mother and daughter. As we sat there—three generations of Black women—I questioned how each of us was experiencing the movie. How did we relate to the characters? In my mother's case, I wondered what memories of her personal experiences were being evoked. For my daughter, I wondered if she realized what our elders endured so she can have the opportunities and privileges she has today. As for me, I wondered if I could have endured and overcome such adversity with the strength, poise, and dignity those women exuded or if I would have folded under the pressure. And while there were numerous points of enlightenment and empowerment throughout the movie, one thing stood out to me regarding the way things were then and the way they are now.

Dorothy Vaughan, played by Octavia Spencer, was a mathematician who led an all-African American woman team of mathematicians who were called "computers." They performed calculations for multiple areas of work at NASA and its predecessor, the National Advisory Committee for Aeronautics (NACA), including during the space race, which was the period covered in Hidden Figures. When she learned the agency was bringing in digital computers, she taught herself how to operate them; she was a self-taught computer programmer. But she didn't stop there. She shared her knowledge with all the women who were under her leadership and fought for them and their White counterparts to receive the positions and pay they deserved.

Mrs. Vaughan could have learned everything she needed to know to advance as the digital age dawned while leaving other women—Black and White—behind. But she didn't. She was not content with being the only person with her level of knowledge or with her position, for which she had to fight to be recognized officially. She found a way to take others with her so they wouldn't find themselves on the sidelines as digital computers replaced human computers at NASA. According to an article published by NASA, when asked about her experiences, she said "I changed what I could, and what I couldn't, I endured" (Vitug, 2017). When you are comfortable, but not content, you do everything you can to change everything you can toward MAKING A DIFFERENCE. You become a gateway rather than a gatekeeper.

4

FIND YOUR VOICE—
AND USE IT

*"If you're afraid to use your voice,
give up your seat at the table."*

FIRST LADY MICHELLE OBAMA

Each of us is unique. Every individual has unique perspectives shaped by their backgrounds, circumstances, and experiences. Each of us has a "voice" that can be used to make a difference. And by voice, I'm not only referring to the audible sound produced by the vocal cords. Often, people who speak the most and the loudest have the least valuable things to say. On the contrary, some who speak the least or are least audible make the most profound contributions. So, finding one's voice is less about how much we say and more about what we say and ultimately, what we do. Discovering—and using—our voice is about the value we each add by bringing our uniqueness into the situations we encounter. It's speaking up for what is right. It's using our power, privilege, authority, and influence to empower others and to effect change.

MORE THAN WORDS CAN SAY

One of the most inspirational, motivational, and impactful people I know is Logan Prickett. A life-altering medical event occurred when he was a teen, resulting in Logan losing his sight, his mobility, and literally losing his voice so that he currently cannot speak above a whisper. I say currently because I am believing with Logan and his family that God will heal and restore him.

Despite the limitations he faces, Logan has "used his voice" to help others in a way that I believe will change the world. Along with Dr. Ann Gulley and Jordan Price, he co-created Process-Driven Math (PDM), which is an audio-based method for teaching and assessing mathematics to ensure accessible and equitable learning opportunities for students who are blind or who have low vision (Gulley, Smith et al, 2017; Gulley, 2021). There is also a version of PDM that has been visually adapted for sighted learners with print-related disabilities such as dyslexia (Philliips, Gulley et al, 2018). Students who have no disabilities benefit from the reduced cognitive load PDM presents as well. Logan co-created and worked with the team to adapt PDM for the mathematics courses in his curriculum, and by doing so, he paved the way for others to succeed. Logan graduated with his bachelor's degree in psychology in four years. At the time I'm writing this, he is now a graduate student, and is still MAKING A DIFFERENCE.

Logan Prickett is currently blind yet is a young man who is full of vision. His vision is for people with disabilities to have full access to educational, research, employment, and recreation opportunities. While accommodations are great, and welcomed, his vision is for universal design to be broadly applied so that facilities, technologies, and outdoor environments are accessible to people with all types of disabilities to reduce the need for accommodations. Logan Prickett cannot currently speak above a whisper, yet his voice resonates for all to hear. He uses his voice to inform some and to remind others that even though some of us have limitations—in our cases, physical limitations—we still have numerous capabilities. People with disabilities have a great deal to offer in all disciplines of study and all areas of professional practice, and Logan advocates and serves as a living, vocal testimony for necessary change in the way disabled people are perceived. Logan cannot currently walk, yet he is paving pathways for true equity for people with disabilities. His vision and voice converge to produce action. Logan currently cannot fully use his hands, yet he touches the lives of everyone he encounters. He certainly has touched—and continues to touch mine.

JOURNEY OF SELF DISCOVERY

My "voice" is something I discovered pretty late in life. I've always actively pursued what I was passionate about in my career—teaching and creating programs to help students succeed in engineering, giving particular attention to overcoming barriers to success for students from various minoritized and marginalized backgrounds. I've always worked to make sure programs didn't overlook people like me—people who don't "look" like prospective engineers on paper—but I was rarely vocal about it. This was something I did because it had purpose and I enjoyed doing it. I was MAK-ING A DIFFERENCE in people's lives yet didn't necessarily recognize it as such.

In 2013, I visited the NSF to interview for a program director position in the Division of Undergraduate Education (DUE). As required for most interviews in academia and other research-related jobs, I had to give a "job talk," which is generally a presentation of one's research background, accomplishments, and vision. To tell you the truth, most job talks I've attended are incredibly boring; the candidate is in front of the room for an hour using a death-by-PowerPoint presentation to run down their resume and share technical details of their research with little or no ability or desire to appear human or make human connections.

I approached my job talk a bit differently. I started by handing out a one-page summary of the key results of my NSF-funded projects and let the attendees know I was open to questions about them. I then started my presentation. The first thing I said was, "If you didn't notice, I'm a Black woman with a disability." They laughed. This gave me a bit more comfort with the audience. Then, instead of reciting my degrees, academic and administrative appointments, and research accomplishments, I told my story.

I spent the early years of my childhood in a lower-income household. We were not in poverty, but we were not quite middle class. I didn't realize it at the time because I don't ever recall being in need; but, in talking to my mother as I got older, I came to learn about a lot of things she went without and the sacrifices she had to make for us to live. Neither of my parents were college graduates when I was growing up. My mom had attended college but left to go to work full-time. I don't even think my dad graduated from high school. My parents divorced when I was eight. My mom remarried when I was 12, but I still felt like I was single-parented because she was the one who was all-hands-on-deck with both my brother, Travis, and me.

I had no obvious interest in STEM at all. I didn't participate in any STEM camps or other activities in high school. I had been in gifted and talented programs from second through eighth grades, but by the time I got to eighth grade and then to high school—forget all that gifted and talented stuff—what I know now as stereotype threat hit me so hard that I became average at best. I attended one of the top high schools in the country at that time, not because I was a stellar student, but because I wanted to be in its jazz band. I auditioned and got in, which was not something that first-year students typically did. I had mediocre to average high school grades. My last math class in high school was Algebra 2 and I got a D in that.

I graduated high school in three years not because I was a stellar student, but because I'd met all the requirements, even with my unimpressive performance. My grade point average was 2.96 (on a 4.0 scale) and my honors music courses contributed to much of that. My plan was to major in music and foreign languages in college because that's what I loved; that's where I excelled. My mother convinced me to try engineering. There were no counselors, teachers, or anyone in my school who ever suggested I consider engineering or any other STEM major.

I did not fit the mold of most people's idea of a future engineer. Yet there I was, in the midst of an interview at NSF—an engineering Ph.D. holder and licensed Professional Engineer nearly 20 years into an outstanding career as an engineering educator. Shaped by my past experiences, my work in higher education has focused on making sure other "Yvettes" don't fall through the cracks—or crevasses—because they don't have "Geraldines" at home to challenge their lack of self-efficacy or to challenge the people and the systems they face that tell them they are not "engineering material."

The other thing I talked about during that presentation was that when I was growing up, my aunt—my mom's sister, Tee Myrt—taught at the Louisiana School for the Visually Impaired (LSVI) and my grandmother, Eunice, was a dorm mother there. My cousin, Andrea, and I spent a lot of time at LSVI when we were growing up, hanging out with students who were blind or had low vision. We played music together, we watched TV together, we did whatever—together. And what I came to realize was, except for those who had multiple disabilities that may have been even more severe, those students could do everything I could do—except see. I used those personal experiences to frame how I wanted to make sure that NSF programs created opportunities to advance the potential of and remove barriers for people from all marginalized identities, including those with visible and invisible disabilities, in engineering and other STEM fields.

When I was at NSF, the Deputy Division Director in DUE at the time, Dr. Don Millard, told me something on the order of, "You know you can say things that other people can't say in ways others can't say them. Other people can say them, but they will be received differently coming from you." And that was when it clicked to me that I'd been doing things all along, but I hadn't been vocal, in the literal sense. It was time for me to change this because I did have a voice. I had a platform that I didn't have previously. I was in a position that could help effect change at a scale that I'd never imagined. And what I had to say, indeed, had value. I haven't shut up or stopped doing since!

YOU'VE FOUND YOUR VOICE, NOW WHAT?

That journey of discovery is how I met Logan, Ann, Jordan, and the rest of "Team Logan." During my last year at NSF, I attended a webinar hosted by the University of Washington's Disabilities, Opportunities, Internetworking, and Technology (DO-IT) center, which is a go-to resource for accessibility and universal design in STEM education. During the webinar, the team described how they came together to create

PDM. Logan shared his story and the possibility of larger implications, as he recognized there were others who did not have the tools they needed to succeed in mathematics. Typically, I would sign into professional development webinars such as this using my university email address; however, that day I signed in with my NSF email address. Months later I learned why God had me do it that way.

Ann Gulley had received a list of webinar attendees from DO-IT, and when she came across the NSF email address, she decided to reach out. After speaking with her, I felt the world needed to know what was going on in Montgomery, Alabama regarding mathematics accessibility. The closest I could come was using my influence to organize a visit for The Logan Project team to share PDM with our staff. The crowd was not as large as I desired, but it was large enough. Everyone in the room was moved by Logan's story, impressed by the team's huge accomplishments with small internal grants, and many grew impassioned about mathematics accessibility. For days, people stopped by my office to thank me for inviting them and asked if there was anything they could do to support the team's work. I helped them arrange meetings with program officers to discuss various funding opportunities. Again, I didn't have to say much. In this case, using my "voice" was about leveraging my professional network to help the team meet and connect with others who were able to support their work. Later, after leaving NSF, I had the added privilege of joining "Team Logan" and helping to advance their work.

SILENCE SPEAKS VOLUMES

What's the point of having a "seat at the table" if we can't—or won't—use it to make a positive difference? This is one reason why inclusion is so important; diversity, which translates as representation, is of little benefit without having different voices and perspectives included so they can make a difference.

Diversity cannot be achieved or sustained without the building blocks of justice, equity, and inclusion. Starting with justice as the foundational block, we must identify and eradicate policies and practices that have created and exacerbated inequities in our academic and workplace environments, as well as in society as a whole. Building upward from there, the next block is equity, which focuses on treating people with dignity, respect, and fairness. Just above equity is inclusion, which ensures that different voices and perspectives are heard, valued, and incorporated on par with others and are not minoritized, even if small in number. Finally, the top block is diversity, which is the desired representation of multiple and intersectional identities that reflect our whole society. Picture these blocks stacked as described from bottom to top with justice as the foundation. If justice is taken away, equity, inclusion, and diversity cannot stand. If equity is not there, inclusion and diversity will topple over. We cannot achieve and sustain diversity without each building block being in place.

Sometimes exclusion happens when people's voices are silenced because of systemic barriers. Other times, people silence themselves, refusing to get involved in things they believe will not impact them directly or because they have been silenced so much, they refuse to speak. Both can be detrimental.

I've experienced having people in authority who did not use their power or influence to advocate for me when I was not in a position to do so myself. In some cases, these have been people who shared at least one of my identities. I'll share one instance but will be intentionally vague on details. Interestingly, the person began as a strong advocate, making sure I was aware of and poised to take advantage of an upcoming opportunity and providing pointers as I went through the process. Somewhere along the way, I ran into a barrier—one that was within their power to help mitigate—and they were silent. Now, don't get me wrong. I didn't expect an easy road or for someone to carry me over the proverbial finish line. I fully expected to earn my way into the opportunity on my own merit, not based on who I knew.

The problem was an inequity that surfaced in the system, equivalent to the rules changing in the middle of the game. This person, though they did not create the barrier, had the ear and the trust of the person who did and could have called it out for what it was—speaking up for what was right, regardless of the outcome for me. While it was troublesome that they were silent when I needed them to speak, what was more painful was that they turned the tables on me, complete with minimizing what I'd experienced and questioning my response to the inequitable treatment (which, in this case was my choosing to "go silent" in a different sense). There's a saying that actions speak louder than words. This person's inaction, their silence when they could have made a difference, spoke volumes to me.

I've also silenced myself after having my voice minimized and marginalized to the extent that I chose not to "speak." During one of my many career transitions, I attempted to help the team for a project I was leading make progress toward the next steps so they wouldn't miss a beat during the change. One of the team members (who had a multi-year track record of proving to be an antagonist to me), repeatedly insisted that the team wait until a new leader took the helm before any further actions were taken. While I appreciated the importance of the new leader having their fingerprint on the project, it was taking longer than expected to identify someone. Because I understood the constraints we faced due to funding agency expectations, I felt the need to keep the ball rolling until a new team leader was there to pick it up, with hopes the transition would be as smooth as possible.

The antagonist's persistent insistence and the silence of other team members coupled with my past experiences caused me to go silent. I completely shut down. Disconnected. I recall thinking (and sharing with people I trust) that I didn't care if the project went to hell in a handbasket at that point. I was done. I was content with leading the part of the project that transitioned with me to make sure that it succeeded, even if all else failed.

I'll be honest. I harbored quite a bit of resentment for some time. And you know what? I was wrong to do that. The project struggled and other people suffered as a result. I set a poor example for younger professionals I was mentoring at the time. All that, plus it had absolutely no impact on my antagonist. This was a person who could never see or acknowledge they were wrong. My mom has always taught me that two wrongs don't make a right. Reflecting on and following my mother's wisdom, I realized I needed to think about the bigger picture—the project's goals—and deal with myself (not the other individual). In doing so, I broke my silence by extending an offer to help the team. It's important to note that I did so without sacrificing my self-care. I was able to insulate myself from the toxicity and was happy to reconnect with the team and provide input to help move things forward toward the project's success.

THE LONE VOICES

When leading trainings for my clients on workplace climate and culture, I caution leaders to be attentive to the voices that show up in isolation or in small numbers. I've had conversations with young Black engineers, often the only folks in their positions at work, who have shared how they've faced marginalization in a number of different ways. Some have experienced supervisors diminishing their credentials while celebrating those of others, even though the latter were lesser. Others have been completely disregarded by contractors and staff within their organizations. I can't tell you the number of women engineers, especially women of color, who have experienced folks requesting to speak with the person in charge when they were the lead engineers on a project.

We often suffer in silence. Sadly, many of us have navigated cultures of inequity for so long we believe it's normal. It's difficult for many to speak up and speak out against those inequities, especially early in their careers, because of fear of the response—or lack thereof. This is especially true for those who are the "only" or the "first" in their departments, units, or positions. Will we be flagged as a "troublemaker" and have that label create more barriers for us? Will we be accused of "playing the race card" when we point out racial inequities? Some of us shoulder the burden for the entire population of folks who share our identities, recognizing that if we make any misstep, it might give our employers an excuse not to hire any more [fill in the identity group] because we didn't work out.

Sometimes when we decide to speak up we're faced with responses like, "No one else has said anything about that." Could it be that because we are the only [fill in the identity group(s)], we are the only one having this experience, and thus the only one who can bring it to light? I've had to become comfortable with being the only person speaking up about certain things. Hearkening to Don Millard's words, I ask myself, "If I don't say it, who will?"

Sometimes leaders believe because they have one or two women or individuals from minoritized racial and ethnic identities in their organizations that neither racism nor sexism could be present. Thus, when a person of color—especially a woman of color—raises a concern or complains about unequal or inequitable treatment the response they are met with is silence, inaction, minimization, or gaslighting. The result is emotional, physical, psychological, and career harm.

This illustrates why intersectionality is important as we address inequities in academia, in the workforce, and in society at large. Disparities in experiences and outcomes are amplified for folks who hold multiple marginalized and/or minoritized identities. This is also why we cannot rely solely on quantitative data from climate surveys and employment statistics. When we don't show up in sufficient numbers, our responses are excluded. Our voices don't count. It is necessary to collect, analyze, and report qualitative data so our stories are heard and used to improve policies and practices.

BEYOND THE BOX CHECKING

Organizations are striving to increase diversity amongst their employees, especially those from minoritized identities, which is good, but insufficient on its own because it is often a "box-checking" exercise that celebrates tokenism and twokenism while doing absolutely nothing to address the systemic problems that create and continue to perpetuate minoritization and marginalization. It is imperative that leaders are willing to take those hard looks in the mirror—the ones that reveal the good, the bad, and the ugly in our organizations. We must take the deep dives that go beyond head counting to examine what people are experiencing, and most importantly, why, so we can then address the root causes of the problems in a strategic way. Without doing this, we cannot—and will not change.

What is equally important is making sure the right folks are hired, regardless of identity, because it is the people in the organization who establish the culture and climate of the organization. It's the people who create a culture of silence in the face of suffering, or who create a culture of action that prevents it. It's the people who cultivate a climate that makes the organization one of the best or one of the worst places to work. And what those people look like, how they identify, and who they are at both the surface and the deepest levels includes a wide range of folks—good and bad.

There's a saying, "All skin folks ain't kinfolks." I've worked with women who are toxic when it comes to other women. I've worked with Black people who are barriers to other Blacks. And I've worked with White men who have been strong advocates and accomplices. Hiring women, people of color, or others from minoritized identities to "get the numbers up" without paying attention to additional attributes can be problematic. What's critically important is that we evaluate all individuals to determine how they might contribute to, or how they might seek to tear down or obstruct, the equitable and inclusive environments we are striving to cultivate—if that is, indeed, what we're striving to do.

EVEN WHEN NO ONE SEEMS TO BE LISTENING

The sad truth is that even when you find and use your voice, some folks won't listen. Some will not hear you; some do not want to hear you. Others will attempt to minimize what you have to say and try to block your efforts to disrupt and eradicate barriers to equity and justice. You can't let that get in the way of you speaking the truth and standing up for what is right.

I was in a meeting where we were discussing proposed changes that would impact civil engineering programs globally. The meeting included faculty members and practitioners from all over. One of the people on the call was solidly against what we were proposing, which was to include principles of diversity, equity, and inclusion in civil engineering curricula. Given that the work of civil engineers focuses so strongly on society and has a tremendous impact on societal outcomes—good and bad—our team found this to be important to the education of future civil engineers. The adversary on the call began by asserting that equity produces discrimination.

I listened carefully to understand the basis of their beliefs, which sadly, too many people hold. I realized they did not understand what equity is, so I shared a definition with examples from academia and data-driven examples of inequitable outcomes of civil engineering designs that result in life-or-death situations for people based on race, socioeconomic status, and disability. For example, research shows wheelchair users are 36% more likely to be killed in accidents than other pedestrians (Kraemer and Benton, 2015). This is because of inadequacies in civil infrastructure. A colleague from industry shared how their company had been working to overcome inequities as well.

After about 10 minutes of discussion, the nay-sayer replied by saying, "I heard everything you said, but you're still not going to change my mind."

When you encounter folks like that—folks who will argue against reality even when there is an overwhelming amount of evidence contrary to everything they are asserting—there's nothing you can do except hope they are few and far between so they are hurdles, rather than barriers, to the progress you are trying to make. In this case, there was only one other person out of about 15-20 on the call who was in the adversary's "Amen" corner. (Interestingly, it was someone who had blatantly disrespected me in public just a few years before while we were in a meeting). Fortunately, we were able to move our efforts to the next step despite their opposition.

I was watching a rerun of the TV show A Different World recently. It was the episode in which Dwayne Wayne (played by the exceptionally handsome Kadeem Hardison) was running for student government president and Rev. Jessie Jackson was visiting the campus for an event. Dwayne had become discouraged because while he wanted to focus on the serious issues—funding, scholarships, etc.—his opponent, and seemingly everyone else at Hillman, wanted to focus on less serious things (Homecoming parties and concerts). He shared his decision to drop out of the race during a conversation at Col. Taylor's home. Rev. Jackson shared his experiences in student government at North Carolina A&T, including some that others would consider failures. Amongst the eloquent words he spoke to encourage Dwayne, he said, "A man can't be heard if he stops talking."

Regardless of whether people listen or not, we must use our voice—our positions, our privileges, our insights, our networks, our influence—to bring awareness to problems that need to be solved and successes that need to be celebrated. If we don't say it, who will? When we are in positions of power to make changes for the better and we don't do it, what good are we? When we hear the outcries of people who are being harmed in our organizations and remain silent, either because of conflict avoidance or because they are a "lone voice," we are just as guilty as those who are inflicting the harm. When we do not use our voice—for good—we miss the opportunity of MAKING A DIFFERENCE within our spheres of influence.

5

IT'S OKAY TO GET ANGRY

*"Sometimes you have to get angry
to get things done."*

ANG LEE

People act as if we're supposed to operate in, or worse, endure systems of oppression without getting angry. That's just not possible, nor is it a reasonable expectation. Anger is an authentic and valid emotion that manifests in response to stressors we encounter in our personal and professional environments. Superminds Platforms, on their website psychguides.com (2022) states, "Stress, financial issues, abuse, [adverse] social or familial situations, and overwhelming requirements on your time and energy can all contribute to the formation of anger." There's a verse in the Bible that teaches "In your anger do not sin" (Ephesians 4:26). So, it's okay to be angry; what matters is how we handle that anger. Are we using anger to fuel fires with no intention of extinguishing them? Or are we using our anger to make a difference?

THE LABEL

Most people have heard—and many of us have experienced—the "angry Black woman" or "angry Black man" trope. Researchers have explained how "racialized anger bias" results in Black people's emotions frequently being mistaken for anger, even when we are not angry. This is harmful in educational settings, as it leads to disparities in disciplinary outcomes for Black children (Halberstadt et al, 2020). It can be a matter of life and death when Black people's anger—real or perceived—is translated by law enforcement officers as a threat. We have seen time and time again how unarmed Black people are considered threats that need to be neutralized by deadly force while non-Black people who commit murder and have their weapons in-hand are either taken into custody unharmed, or in some cases, are celebrated by police.

In his book *How to Be an Antiracist*, Dr. Ibram X. Kendi (2019) describes an encounter with a teacher who had repeatedly marginalized students of color in her class. He became angry when he witnessed how she'd treated a Black girl in his class. He was young at the time and wasn't sure how to handle the justifiable emotions he was experiencing. Though he was silent, by refusing to engage the young Kendi "used his voice" to confront and challenge the inequities his classmate faced. It took a while for the teacher to realize that something was wrong, and when she did, she interpreted his withdrawal from class activities and refusal to move on with "business as usual" as a behavioral problem that required discipline. She never acknowledged her wrongdoing; she faced no consequences for the racially biased system she had created that oppressed students of color in her class.

CHOOSING YOUR BATTLES

I have learned over the years to be conscientious about how I handle the anger that arises in me when I encounter the foolishness of inequities and -isms. First, I listen to try to understand. Then I do one of a few things. I might explain if I believe the person has a misunderstanding that can be clarified. Sometimes, I speak out boldly to call out the problematic speech or behavior. Other times, I say nothing—at least not right away; I take time to think strategically about how to best address the situation. I've always been taught to choose my battles; sometimes I forego engaging in smaller "battles" to win larger "wars."

I was in a meeting during which the subject of faculty hiring came up. This is a common conversation across the U.S.; institutions are trying to determine the best strategies for recruiting, hiring, and retaining faculty from minoritized identities, which also has a bearing on student recruitment and success. In this meeting, someone made a statement that was disparaging to HBCUs. Honestly, I don't believe they understood what they were saying; in the course of the conversation, they made a comparison that positioned HBCUs as inferior to other institutions.

Intent and impact often diverge; good (or even neutral) intentions can produce negative impacts. The former doesn't supersede the latter. I took a deep breath and decided not to respond in the moment (though I had been vocal about other things in that meeting). Intended or unintended, these types of slights and biases have the impact of limiting our efforts toward diversity, equity, and inclusion in our academic institutions and in our professions, with engineering being amongst the hardest to change.

Later, I ran into a colleague—a White man who has proven himself to be an advocate and accomplice for advancing equity. He was also in that meeting, where the conversation had taken a deep, racially focused turn. I'd chimed in at selected points, calmly yet firmly expressing my points of view.

He commented, "I don't see how you don't get angry." I responded, "Oh, I get angry. I get extremely angry, but I must choose how and when to respond."

In the case of the deficit framing of HBCUs in our meeting, I continued to listen, as the words that were spoken let me know who—and what—I was dealing with so I could use that in a bigger, longer-term strategy to help address the underlying issues rather than have a moment in a meeting and risk the angry Black woman trope—"the label."

What my colleague, my accomplice, realized and acknowledged at that moment was something I and countless others have known for years. As Black people, especially Black women, we must calculate our responses carefully. Many times, our White counterparts, especially men, can blow up, curse people out, and say whatever they want—however they want—and not only avoid negative consequences, but also be celebrated. Their outbursts are viewed as expressions of passion. If we even speak loudly or assert ourselves in situations, some folks will say they feel threatened, that we're insubordinate, or give us "the label."

TEACHABLE MOMENTS

During my time at the National Science Foundation (NSF), one of my responsibilities was to manage panels where external folks, usually academicians, discussed research proposals and made recommendations for program officers to consider as we decided which projects we should recommend for award or decline.

> *Disclaimer: What I'm about to share are my perspectives based on personal experience. The opinions, conclusions, and recommendations expressed are mine and do not necessarily reflect the views of the National Science Foundation.*

During one panel, reviewers were discussing a proposal from an HBCU and one panelist started their part of the discussion by saying, "I might have an implicit bias here, but..." then proceeded with their evaluation of the proposal. The panelist berated the proposal—saying what the institution wouldn't be able to do, what "those students" were incapable of, and spewing out all sorts of negativity. Being a two-time alumna of an HBCU and knowing the disproportionate distribution of research funding to HBCUs across all federal agencies, I got angry as the panelist continued with the rant. But I let them speak. I wanted to see how deeply they would dig their hole.

> When you can start a statement with the words, "I might have an implicit bias..." it's NOT an implicit bias! One of the biggest barriers to change is that people use "implicit bias"—which is real—as a crutch, a catch-all, and an excuse to ignore the very real explicit biases that are often pervasive in our institutions and workplaces.

Another reviewer interrupted to point out that the panelist had not raised any of the same questions or concerns about other proposals, hinting at the first panelist's obvious bias against the subject proposal. NSF goes to great lengths to ensure an equitable review process, which includes making sure panelists are aware of potential biases and that they have ways to mitigate them should they arise.

I grew angry as the panelist went on. I stepped in, reiterating the other panelist's point about asking different questions regarding this proposal than those asked of others, and in my anger, chose to use this as a teachable moment. This panelist had a poor image of HBCUs and the graduates they produce. I spent the next several minutes very calmly—and very firmly—sharing my background, including that I was not only an HBCU alumna, but that I had also taught at one for 12 years. I then talked about the distorted view of "merit" that overlooks and excludes a wide range of folks. The last thing I recall pointing out was that if I limited myself based on how other people saw—or did not see—my potential, I wouldn't have been sitting where I was that day; in a position to help determine funding priorities for the nation's premier STEM research agency.

I don't know if I changed that reviewer's mind; in retrospect, I'm sure I didn't. However, there were a few other people in the room, and who knows if someone else might have been thinking what that reviewer had the gall to say aloud. I hoped that what I shared enlightened not only that individual but also other reviewers and that they would think about this if they were in a similar situation in the future. And then I used my "voice" in another way. I recommended that proposal for funding; it was a darn good proposal and NSF made the award.

SEEKING WISE COUNSEL

Wise counsel (emphasis on "wise") is essential to good decision making, especially when managing anger. A few years ago, during an impromptu pre-event conversation with renowned educator, speaker, trainer, and mentoring expert Dr. Howard G. Adams, he gave me a piece of career advice I have held onto. He said, "You always need someone to have a bad day with." We weren't discussing anger at the time; we were just discussing the reality of challenges—hurdles and barriers— that we encounter in the workplace.

Rather than keep our thoughts and emotions bottled up, we need to be able to express them, and do so in a way and with someone that allows us to be authentic, without fear of negative consequences. It also needs to be fruitful so it doesn't result in a pity party, oppression Olympics, or a general gripe session. In the workplace, I have been blessed to find colleagues—and friends—whom I can trust to give wise counsel. And while we sometimes have gripe sessions, we always ask, "So what are we going to do?" We do our best to leave the conversation with an action plan.

Often when I am disturbed or angered by situations I encounter, I discuss my possible responses and courses of action with a couple of folks who are closest to me—my mom and one of my best friends. These are two people whom I trust and who speak the truth to me, even if it's not what I want to hear at the time. Both of them provide guidance rather than tell me what I should do or what they would do in the situation.

My mom is fantastic at helping me to see things from multiple angles, then asking me, "So what are you going to do?" My friend is good at talking me down when I'm ready to jump in swinging, which he normally does by asking, "What good is that going to do? What difference will that make?" Even when they are not around, I hear their voices in my head. This forces me to stop—even in my anger—and think strategically about how to handle things. Sometimes, in the moment, the "do nothing" alternative is best. Sometimes it is entirely right to come out swinging. In all cases, I strive to make sure my response—in the moment or delayed—matters so I'm not just angry, I'm M.A.D.—MAKING A DIFFERENCE.

6

BE MINDFUL OF HOW YOU TREAT OTHERS

"We live in a world in which we need to share responsibility. It's easy to say 'It's not my child, not my community, not my world, not my problem.' Then there are those who see the need and respond. I consider those people my heroes."

FRED ROGERS

Some people call it Karma. I call it sowing and reaping (Galatians 6:7). I'm a firm believer that whatever seeds we sow will produce their fruit in our lives. If we sow seeds of positivity, we will reap a harvest of good things. If our plantings are negative, we will reap bad things in return. Does this mean good things never happen to people who do bad things, or that bad things never happen to those who do good? Certainly not! Both good and bad happen to everyone. However, when we focus on sowing good seeds, I believe our net return is good, and somehow good finds its way to us even in the midst of negative circumstances.

THE (SEEMINGLY) SIMPLE THINGS

One way I endeavor to sow good seeds is by treating others the way I want to be treated or the way I want those I love and care about to be treated. It's relatively simple, yet a struggle for many. I have observed how some of my colleagues disrespected and devalued some students in their classes or whom they advised. Even before I had a child of my own, and certainly after she was born, I did my best to treat my students with care and respect—whether they were "A" students or they were struggling to maintain good academic standing. I recognized my students were people, and though they were adults, they were somebody's children. I knew one day my child would be someone's student and I wanted her to be treated with dignity, respect, and fairness.

Sometimes treating people with dignity is as simple as recognizing their humanity. When I lived in Virginia, most of the time my greetings of, "good morning" or "good evening" when I entered an occupied elevator in my apartment building were met with blank, unresponsive stares. I wondered why. Were people not accustomed to someone greeting them? Were they so self-absorbed that they could not look down and acknowledge the woman in the wheelchair? Or were there stressors that occupied their minds so much that they didn't even realize they were on an elevator, let alone anyone else? I never knew, but I never stopped, with hopes a kind smile (that my orthodontist, Dr. Moody Alexander, spent a lot of time improving) and a warm greeting might somehow make their day tiny bit better.

I recall speaking with a friend who was annoyed that someone had gone on and on about the challenges they were facing when my friend asked them, "How are you doing?" He, along with many others, will tell you when someone asks how you're doing, it's just a pleasantry; nobody really cares. What if we did care? What if we asked how someone's doing and actually listened? And let's take an even bigger leap. What if we not only listened, but also responded appropriately—with joy when someone's excited; with empathy when someone's struggling; or with another question, "How can I help?" if someone is distressed or in need? Imagine how much of a difference those seemingly small and relatively simple actions would make.

GOOD HOME TRAINING

My grandmother, who we called "Maw Maw," was a person who helped anyone she could. Her doors were always open to anyone. I watched as she fed and nurtured a neighbor who struggled with the disease of alcoholism. She treated him as if he was one of her own children. Whenever any of us showed up with our friends—announced or unannounced—they were always welcomed with open arms (and an open kitchen). No matter how much or how little she had, somehow there was always more than enough to share. This relentless openness to and care for others has been part of our family's upbringing for generations. We refer to it as "good home training."

We lived with Maw Maw for a significant portion of my childhood, and her "good home training" was nearly always on display. Our home was on Highway 415 in Lobdell, a small rural community in Louisiana. When I was very young, the highway was a two-lane corridor that served as a connector between I-10 and Highway 190. It was expanded later to four lanes to meet increased traffic demand.

I recall being at home with Maw Maw one day when a strange car pulled off the highway and down "the ramp" to our house. "The ramp" was our name for the driveway; the elevation of the highway was significantly different from the property, forcing the driveway onto an incline. A middle-aged stranger knocked on the door. Maw Maw approached the door with caution to ask who he was and what he wanted. I stood at a comfortable distance behind her—close enough to her to jump in if something went to the left; close enough to the red rotary dial phone on the red-tiled kitchen wall to call the police, if I had to.

The man said he wasn't feeling well and asked for help. My grandmother opened the door, placed a chair on the front stoop for him to sit, and we called 911. An ambulance came and took the man away, but I don't recall what happened after that. I'm certain someone came to retrieve his vehicle at some point.

Sometime later (maybe weeks, perhaps months; I'm not sure), once again an unfamiliar car came down the ramp and a stranger knocked on the door. It was the same man. This time, he was coming to thank my grandmother for saving his life. We learned he'd had a heart attack the day he first came to our door. The chance he took driving up to the home of a stranger was literally a life-or-death matter for him. There were other driveways he could have entered; other homes he could have approached. I believe God ordered his steps that day and sent him to my Maw Maw—a woman who treated everyone well—and she made sure he got the help he needed.

I've carried on the tradition of "good home training" in raising my own daughter. I can't go anywhere with Amber without someone stopping us to comment on how beautiful she is and to ask if she's a model. She's 19 now, and this has been happening since she was a toddler. When people made those comments back then, and throughout her early childhood, I regularly stopped to remind her (after she'd said "thank you" and they'd moved on) that she was, indeed, beautiful on the outside, and that it was even more important to be beautiful on the inside. That's a lesson I'm proud she has not only remembered and embraced but has also embodied throughout her life.

We moved to Virginia when Amber was in fifth grade. One day, I received a phone call from her school that took me through a range of emotions—fear, confusion, anger, and ultimately, pride. I can't recall if it was one of her teachers or someone from the office. The caller told me that everything was fine, but (in comes the fear) there had been a time that day during which they were unable to locate Amber (in comes the confusion and anger). She had somehow disappeared during lunch, and no one knew where she was. I was flummoxed. How could my 10-year-old disappear from a confined space (a cafeteria) without someone noticing?

When they found her, she was in another classroom. She'd decided to forego lunch and chose to spend her time reading to a disabled kindergartener instead. That's when the pride kicked in. While I was frustrated with the school that this happened, I was thankful that she was safe and pleased that she'd chosen to give of herself to help someone else. When she got home, we had a conversation about the importance of getting permission to leave places she's expected to be; however, I also spent a great deal of time commending her on her selflessness.

Fast forward to her eleventh grade year. A few months before the world became aware of the COVID-19 pandemic, we were in Sydney, Australia. My mom, Amber and I had taken a water taxi to explore a shopping area on an overcast day with an intermittent drizzle. We were strolling along, minding our business, and Mom and I were talking. Amber stopped suddenly. I asked her what was wrong. She said, "That girl back there. Mommy, I think she needs help."

"What girl?" I asked. Neither Mom nor I had noticed anyone. Amber pointed, and sure enough, we had passed a young woman sitting next to a pillar supporting the structure we were walking (and in my case, rolling) under. We paused a moment to observe, trying to discern whether she was just taking a load off or if she was someone who was, indeed, in need. I'm hesitant to approach strangers, so I wanted to gather as many visual clues as I could before deciding what to do next. Amber insisted that we go back to check on her, and Mom and I agreed that we should.

I approached her with a smile, greeted her and asked if she was okay. She said she was. I asked if she was sure, and she said yes. Then I asked her if she needed anything. I let her know my daughter was concerned about her well-being. She thanked us and insisted she was okay, so we continued our journey. I was proud that my daughter was able to sense the possibility of someone needing our help, that she was bold enough to say something, and persistent enough to make sure we listened to her and followed through. Even though she didn't need our help, I hope the young woman was encouraged in knowing there are strangers in this world willing to come to her aid with love and compassion.

Maw Maw taught her children and their children to do as she did—reach out a helping hand to anyone who needs it, and share whatever we have, regardless of how much we have to give. I'm thankful for these generational lessons, examples, and values I'm now able to share with my daughter and that I'm able to exhibit in my daily life.

Of course, not everyone is comfortable approaching strangers, and that's understandable. Without unmistakable signs of an emergency, I would be hesitant to welcome a stranger into my home, especially given the times we now live in. It is wise to exercise caution with strangers because there are predators who seek prey by pretending to be in need.

There are numerous ways we can extend care and support to others. We can give our time and talents to help teach or tutor. Pick up a few extra non-perishable items whenever we buy groceries and donate them to a local food pantry. Show up to serve the homeless population or a local charity throughout the year, instead of waiting until November and December. Go through our bookshelves and our closets each season and donate items—the good items—we are not using to people who need them. We can teach our children to give by having them identify a toy to donate whenever they receive a new one.

Make a phone call or send an email to introduce a colleague to someone who can help them advance toward their goals. Spend time coaching folks who are interested in pursuing a career path similar to ours. There are always people who have needs in areas where we have abundance, and this is not limited to material resources. Sometimes the best things we can share are our time, our knowledge, and our influence.

WATCH OUT FOR TRAPS

Unfortunately, not everyone has good home training. Some folks set an agenda that benefits themselves and they don't care or consider who gets hurt as they advance that agenda.

Dealing with these types of people, you have to have your guard up so you don't fall into the traps they set for you or inadvertently become a co-conspirator in traps they're setting for others. At the same time, you can't allow yourself to get on their level by meeting their evil with evil. As First Lady Michelle Obama said, "When they go low, we go high." As God said, "Do not be overcome by evil, but overcome evil with good" (Romans 12:21). It's easier said than done, but needs to be done nonetheless.

It's not easy is to treat others with dignity when they don't reciprocate, or worse, they disrespect you. Sometimes being mindful about how you treat others requires a tightrope walk between self-preservation and perseverance, especially when dealing with an impudent antagonist who is in a position of authority over you. If this person is an employer, you have to persevere in order to do your job and keep your job until it's time for you to move to the next stage of your journey. But that doesn't mean that you ignore self-care. You have to shield your personal and professional well-being from some people.

Years ago, I had a supervisor who was crafty. Let's call them "Chris." Chris knew where the lines were between right and wrong and walked them ever so carefully so they could appear to be on the right side at all times. I'm nearly certain that had there been even a possibility of negative consequences, they had a plan for whom they would shove over the line and under the bus. I believe this wholeheartedly because of an experience I had with a project they asked me to lead in collaboration with a colleague from another department.

Chris specified the general outcomes they desired and asked us to develop the nuts and bolts of the plans and strategies for accomplishing those goals. Having deep knowledge about policies, practices, budgetary constraints, and other factors that would impact the project, my colleague and I crafted the plan to deliver most of what Chris had asked for. Doing *exactly* what they asked would have been out of step with some significant policies and practices and could have resulted in severe consequences. And whose fingerprints and names would have been all over it? Mine and my colleague's.

We presented our plan in a meeting with Chris and my colleague's supervisor, and Chris was not happy because it did not meet all of their expectations. It wasn't until they blew up in (and after) that meeting that I realized we didn't have a paper trail or electronic trail for what they were asking us to do. Surely, had we followed through, we would have exposed ourselves to a level of risk that could have cost us our jobs— or worse. We dropped the project and moved on. I had to protect myself while also maintaining a working relationship with my supervisor, recognizing, and as hard as it was, respecting their position of authority.

I had already developed a distrust for my supervisor because of their prior actions. On another occasion, Chris stopped in my office for a chat. Drop-in conversations were pretty common in our workplace. Often folks would stop and stand at the threshold of an open office door to have a quick chat or to invite colleagues to join them for lunch or a coffee run. Other times, we had relatively short sit-down conversations about a project, an opportunity, or a challenge we were trying to navigate.

What made this drop-in different was its covert nature: Chris came in, asked for a few minutes of my time, and proceeded to sit down and close the door. After exchanging niceties, unscrupulous intentions were slowly revealed. They began by asking me questions about another colleague. I indicated that I had a good working relationship with that person and was curious about where things were headed. Chris probed more, this time with leading questions. They were attempting to get me to say negative things about my colleague. I didn't.

Later that day, a couple of other colleagues and I were together and one asked, "Did Chris stop by your office today?" We discovered we'd all had the same experience. They were going from person to person to dig up dirt on this colleague. Their purpose for doing this was unclear. I'm so happy I didn't feed into it. I said nothing. I was a good ally. Our other two colleagues refused to engage as well. One of them went a step further. They described how they not only refused to throw the target of Chris' inquiries under the bus, but also told Chris they felt what they were doing was inappropriate. That colleague was an accomplice. They not only spoke up to help the target's case, but they also put themselves at risk by speaking truth to power.

Had we given in to Chris' lines of inquiry, they would have used whatever we said against our colleague, and we would have been on the record as having provided details to condemn them. I often wondered what would have happened had we taken the bait and trash talked our colleague with our supervisor. If Chris was trying to use us against someone else, who might they be attempting to use to build up false accusations against us? Proverbs 26:27 states, "Whoever digs a pit will fall into it." We have to not only watch out for traps folks set for us, but also the pits folks will try to drag us into digging for others.

When seeking to build community on teams, employers and facilitators often include trust as a guiding principle or core value. The guidance is often for team members to always assume positive intentions of their colleagues. A word of caution. Trust must be cultivated, earned. It is difficult to build trust, especially among individuals who do not know each other well. It's even harder when there are people on the team who have undermined that trust. And once trust is broken, it's hard, if not impossible, to regain. So, while trust is good and is essential to strong, positive relationships, when it is absent, we must ask why. Then we must take the time to deal with the "why" instead of trying to "fix" the folks who can no longer trust.

LEAD WITH GRACE

I find a lot of practitioners and advocates who strive to advance justice, equity, diversity, and inclusion (JEDI) are combative in their approach to pursuing change. It's okay to be angry, and we have every right to be angry about the inequities and injustices prevalent in our society, workplaces, and academic institutions. The problem is that if we are constantly beating people up, they can't—or won't—listen. The late Supreme Court Associate Justice Ruth Bader Ginsburg said, "Fight for the things that you care about, but do it in a way that will lead others to join you." Think of it like this: people can't do calculus until they grasp key concepts from algebra and geometry; and without a solid foundation in arithmetic, they cannot learn the more advanced subjects.

I can't tell you the number of times I grew frustrated, and even lost it, with my own child when trying to help her with math homework when she was in middle school and high school. After all, I was an "award-winning educator," so certainly my teaching skills were strong. I knew how to present problems within several contexts that should have been relatable to her. Why wasn't she able to get the core concepts so we could move forward?

I was trying to get her ready for calculus by her senior year of high school. Ultimately, when I would raise my voice after asking her the same question three times, she would shut down. Even if she knew the correct answer or the next step, she would refuse to speak because she was afraid of being wrong and the subsequent tongue-lashing that might follow.

I recognized my wrongdoing and apologized to my daughter. It took some time for her to trust that I wouldn't lose patience as I helped her with homework. While I did better, I wasn't perfect. Ultimately, I decided it would be better for me to engage someone else and hired a tutor to help her. In all situations, whether it's with our children, friends, colleagues, or others, it is important to acknowledge when we're wrong. We cannot undo any harm we cause; however, we should do whatever is within our power and ability to help heal the hurt and to make things better from that point forward.

How many times have we seen this happen in other areas of life? Whether it's advancing JEDI and folks miss the mark, teaching a new song to a choir and folks are off-key, or managing a department and a team member misses something important. We are all human. We all mess up. We have to recognize that people are on different points of the learning curve, so we must lead by example and in doing so, extend grace.

I've had times when staff members didn't produce the deliverables expected, either because they misunderstood the assignment or because something unexpected happened. I had two choices in those moments—blow up, scream, and put folks down or figure out what happened, complete the task at hand, and figure out how to do better next time, if possible. Sometimes doing better falls on me—making sure expectations are clear, building in more frequent check-ins, and creating more cushion between internal and external deadlines. Other times it falls on the team member—being coachable so they can course correct and prevent the challenges, if possible (emergencies notwithstanding), asking for help if they run into a hurdle or if they are unclear about the task at hand. In either case, communication and respect are key.

Think about mistakes you've made. How did others treat you? How did you respond? If they beat you up about it, you might have shut down and been hesitant to try again for fear of messing up. If they were patient, you likely felt safe, even after being corrected. Now don't get me wrong. Some people are "repeat offenders" when it comes to negative behaviors, and though they've been corrected and extended grace, they persist in their ways. These aren't mistakes; these are patterns of behavior that need to be met with appropriate consequences. I want to believe that most people want to do better when they make mistakes in most areas of their lives. We just need to stop trying to "teach calculus" to people who are still learning how to do "basic arithmetic."

The bottom line is this: treat others how you want to be treated. Or take yourself out of the equation. How do you want your parents, children, loved ones, and friends to be treated? Would you want a caring fifth grader to take the time to read to your kindergartner who's disabled? If you were a person just beginning to learn something, a staff member whose boss was out to get you, or an individual trying to advance in your professional community—how would you want others to respond to your needs in those moments? What actions would you want others to take to support, sponsor, and champion you? Would you want someone to provide assistance if your life or your loved one's life depended on it? "So in everything, do to others what you would have them do to you…" (Matthew 7:12) are truly words to live by when you are intent on MAKING A DIFFERENCE.

7

LEAVE A LEGACY

"Always leave things better than you found them."

GERALDINE E. JACKSON

My mother taught me something early in life that I still live by to this day. If I had a drink at someone's house, I was taught not only to wash my glass afterward, but if other dishes were in the sink, to wash those as well. If I borrowed a family member's vehicle (which I was encouraged not to do), I was taught to not only replace the gas I used but to fill the tank up and wash the vehicle before returning it. If I was an overnight guest in someone's home, I was taught to get up on the last morning of my stay, strip the bed, wash the sheets, and leave the room spotless. In essence, my mother, Geraldine E. Jackson, taught me to always leave things better than I found them.

We come and go in a lot of different ways every day—into and out of jobs, projects, ministries, and relationships. When we show up in an organization or in people's lives, things should start looking upward because we are there. I am in no way saying that we should display narcissistic behaviors. Rather, when we show up as our best selves—bringing something new and uniquely positive with us—we can truly make a difference. And when we leave, things should be better because we were there.

When we think of someone leaving a legacy, it's often in a morbid sense—looking at what someone leaves behind as they depart this life; oftentimes notoriety or something that has monetary value. In another sense, a legacy is someone who is given special consideration when joining an organization because of a family member's membership or other relationship with that organization. We see this with fraternities, sororities, and with college admissions; applicants are given special consideration because their parents are alumni of a university or are members of an organization.

I like to take elements from both meanings to establish a slightly different spin on legacy. Legacy is about the value we add to an organization and to the lives of the people we touch, whether directly or indirectly. It's about removing, or at least reducing barriers, for not only those who follow in our paths, but also those whose paths are impacted by our actions.

ESTABLISHING VALUE

When I left my tenured associate professorship at Southern University to join UT Arlington (then a PWI, now a Hispanic-Serving Institution) as a non-tenure track senior lecturer, I faced all sorts of nay-sayers. One colleague warned me that, based on his experience (having worked at both Southern and a PWI), going from an HBCU to a PWI would open me up to students questioning my ability and challenging my authority. Another said, "You're not even going to a flagship" and asserted that my colleagues would not respect me because of my non-tenure track position. Still another looked at me completely puzzled and questioned me as if I wasn't making an informed decision.

Now, don't get me wrong. I had folks who were solidly in my corner, expressing their joy for my transition. People like Edith "Ginger" Womack, a Ph.D. student at the time and former classmate and friend who wrote a card wishing me well and calling me her "shero." Dr. Karen Crosby and Dr. Edgar Blevins, my dear friends in mechanical engineering, were excited for me and helped me pack up my home for the move. My students were sad to see me leave, but happy to see I was making a change that was good for me.

Even though I received the positivity with open arms and an open heart, my mind still held on to those negative words. (Isn't it funny how we do that?) I recall thinking, "The first thing I need to focus on when I get there is establishing my value. If they are hiring me as a 'token' Black or have the predisposition to have less respect for me, they'll know better when they see what I bring to the table."

Though I've always sought to make a difference with the things I do, this was the first time I can remember having the explicit thought that I needed to establish my value. I've learned since that this type of "I'll show you" attitude is problematic, as it's rooted in systems of oppression that dictate that people from minoritized and/or marginalized identities must prove our worth, while others are not held to the same standards or expectations. It's something I've been conscious about since that time, and while I still seek to establish value, it comes solely from a place of desiring to improve outcomes for my organizations and the people we serve rather than from the need to build my "street cred."

When I left UT Arlington for my rotation at the NSF, the value I sought to add was more equity and inclusion in the review process and more focus on disability in STEM education. I accomplished that by working with a colleague to revamp the way panels were assigned to one of our division's largest programs to improve equity in the review process, bringing in more Black panelists than I think the division ever saw, introducing industry panelists to review for programs that had strong workforce components, and bringing folks like The Logan Project team to show the possibilities for disabled people in STEM.

When I started my company, one aim was to help institutions—especially predominantly undergraduate institutions, Minority Serving Institutions, and others seeking to advance equity and inclusion—develop competitive proposals for funding opportunities. Through consulting and with grants received through my previous institution, my teams and I have helped teams to acquire roughly $30 million in funding (so far) to support their efforts. The non-monetary value is innumerable. Those funds are reaching students we could never reach personally and generating impacts that we will never know.

While at Rice, I sought to help advance diversity, equity, and inclusion (DEI) in the School of Engineering and at the university more broadly. I recall having a discussion with my dean at the time, who asked me to re-write my job description to include DEI once he learned about my background and accomplishments (he had joined the university a year after I'd joined). I discussed with him the desire to have DEI in my position, but not in my title. We chose to use "Strategic Initiatives" in the title to send the message that DEI was part of our strategy, to be integrated into "business as usual" instead of being siloed and relegated to the margins of our work.

At times, I was met with roadblocks; as a result, I did not accomplish everything I set out to do. However, working with great people at all levels of the institution, we were able to make strong, positive strides that included creating programs and leading research to identify and address barriers to people from racially and ethnically minoritized identities entering the STEM professoriate, leading the development of core values and a code of conduct for the School of Engineering, and helping lead institutional change initiatives.

Before I left—and since I've been at UT Dallas—I received numerous emails communicating how people felt I'd made a difference. One I recall in particular came from one of the other deans on campus. It stood out to me because he said that I was leaving Rice better than I found it. To me, that was my signal. That let me know that I had served my purposes for my season there; that I had acted in accordance with my mother's wisdom.

THERE FOR A PURPOSE

Nothing just happens. I believe everything happens for a reason. I've experienced time and time again how God has ordered my steps, leading me to different opportunities when I had no clue how much they would mean to me—and to others—in the end. Some people seek "a purpose" for their lives. I'm a strong believer that each of our lives is filled with many purposes. The reason for our existence is not limited to just one big thing we are supposed to do before we leave this planet; there are many purposes in the things we do, the people we meet, the places we live, the places we work, and the lives we touch every day.

I remember relocating to a new city for a job. It was nothing short of a miracle how God orchestrated my getting the job and my finding and buying the perfect home for my family. I knew without a doubt that this was set up by God. About a year later, I faced extreme marginalization and minimization on the job, including being told that I needed to "prove myself" to attain an appointment for which I exceeded the qualifications. Prove myself. At that point in my career, it was something I refused to accept; it was something I refused to do. If my experience, accomplishments, credentials, accolades, awards, and honors were not enough, there was nothing else I could do—or would do.

> This is one of those moments I had to suppress my anger. I recall having a conversation with my supervisor on a Friday afternoon and asking him to allow me until Monday to respond because I felt the next thing that would come out of my mouth wouldn't be productive and might get me in trouble. When I returned that Monday, I was able to calmly express my extreme dissatisfaction—and keep my job. A human resources staff member asked if I wanted to take action, expressing that I had grounds. I declined believing there was a larger war to wage and win.

Shortly after this, I received an email from a search firm indicating I'd been nominated for a position as Dean of Engineering at a research university. Mind you, there are two jobs in academia I've never wanted; dean is one of them. Despite this, I entertained a phone call, which led to an interview. I ended up being one of the folks invited for what's called an "airport interview," in which select candidates are flown into town for an in-person interview with the search committee under a shroud of secrecy. My candidacy ended after that, and though I didn't want the job, I was disappointed because I wanted to leave my current job.

God reminded me of all He'd done to get me to where I was. I remembered every detail of how I got to where I was both in that job and in my home. I stopped and I prayed. It was something like, "God, I know you brought me here for a purpose. Please show me what it is I'm here to do and help me do it so I can move on to the next stage of my journey, in Jesus' name." I got my answer, and after I started walking in that purpose, things lined up perfectly to prepare me for that next stage, which was something exceedingly, abundantly above what I could ask or conceive.

We must be careful not to uproot ourselves from where we are planted before it's time. Doing so might cause us to not fulfill our purpose for being there. Had I not stayed where I was planted for that season, I would have missed the opportunity to meet some incredible people who are still part of my life; I would not have gained the tools and assets I needed for my next steps; and I would not have been able to leave a legacy of programming, practices, and policies that resulted in improved equity for a wide range of folks.

This is true in relationships, too. I remember my mom telling me when I was a teen that I would be blessed to have enough true-blue friends that I can count on one hand; and she was right. There's a handful of people who have been in my life since high school and will be for a lifetime; there are others who have come and gone, some more quickly than others. I have gotten to a point that when I meet new people in more than just a passing way, I stop and ask God why.

Why did He make the connection or allow the connection to be made? The selfish part of me wants to ask, "What can this person do for me?" However, I tend to ask instead, "Why did we meet? Is there something I'm supposed to do for this person? How can I add value to this person's life?" Sometimes the answer is clear—there is a need that surfaces that I can help fill (spiritual, educational, emotional, financial, or other); other times, it's not so clear, so I stay on the journey to learn more.

KNOW YOUR WORTH

People sometimes have a way of trying to devalue you, especially when you hold one or more marginalized identities. That's why it's critically important for you to know your worth to the point that you are willing to walk (or roll) away to keep from being walked on (or rolled over).

I had someone reach out to me because they had heard of me and many of the things I'd accomplished, and they wanted to speak with me about a senior-level role in their organization. We had numerous discussions over the course of several months; they courted me hard, and I was interested. We got to the point of talking money. As always, I did my homework.

Because it was a public institution, I was able to look up salary and budget information. When asked what salary I'd accept for the position we'd discussed, I gave them a number that was consistent with others who had roles on a similar level. When I shared the number, I was met with the question, "On what basis?" I'm nearly 100% certain that had I held a different set of identities, I would not have received such a question.

My response was something along the lines of, "On the basis that I have over 20 years of experience with specialized knowledge for what you're asking me to do; and besides, there are entry-level folks in your organization who are earning not much less than what I'm requesting." I stood my ground. They went away with that information and said they'd follow up with me later. When they did, they'd knocked the position down a notch, with me reporting to someone who had a reputation for having others do the work while they took the credit.

I was not willing to accept that; I knew my worth in salary, in capabilities, and in hierarchy. I was willing to stay put rather than take a position with a great appearance knowing that I wouldn't be valued. In the meantime, another opportunity came along where the supervisor knew my worth, and I landed somewhere else altogether.

THE JOURNEY CONTINUES

I often think about what's next on my journey. Part of that includes questioning what legacy I'll leave from my current and future endeavors. And not a legacy for the sake of notoriety, but legacy in the sense of the impact I hope to have. I challenge you to think about the same.

Think about the last "place" you left. This could be a job, a relationship, a place of worship, or another situation. Did you leave it better than you found it? Did things end the way you wanted? What could you have done, if anything, to make things better? What can you do in your current organization or position to add value and pave the way for others who will follow you?

What are those characteristics that make you uniquely you? What are things that come easily to you, and perhaps, not so easily to others? How can you use those to make a positive difference? Recognize that no one else can offer the world what you were created and crafted to bring to it in the way that you have been uniquely gifted to do so. Don't let others quell your individuality by putting you in a box—and don't confine yourself to boxes, either.

Be comfortably discontent with being the "first" or the "only"—comfortable enough to thrive and discontent enough to work with intentionality and purpose on being a gateway and not a gatekeeper for others who will follow you.

Get angry when needed and get something done as a result so you're not just angry, you're M.A.D. (MAKING A DIFFERENCE). Always be mindful of how you treat others, remembering that what you put out into this world has a way of being returned to you.

Listen to what's in your heart. What's the passion that drives you? Identify your spheres of influence and use your voice—your power, your position, your privilege—to make what the late, great Congressman John Lewis called "Good Trouble." In doing all of this, you'll certainly leave a legacy—one of value that positively impacts your workplace, your institution, and all the lives that are reached by your work. One that assures you are MAKING A DIFFERENCE.

REFERENCES

Butrymowicz, S. & Mader, J. (2017). Low academic expectations and poor support for special education students are 'hurting their future'. The Hechinger Report. https://hechingerreport.org/low-academic-expectations-poor-support-special-education-students-hurting-future/

Collins, J. (2001). *Good to great.* Random House Business Books.

Encyclopedia Britannica (2022). Tokenism. In *The Britannica Dictionary.* https://www.britannica.com/dictionary/tokenism

Graziosi, D. (2019). *Millionaire success habits: The gateway to wealth & prosperity.*

Gulley, A. P., Smith, L. A., Price, J. A., Prickett, L. C., & Ragland, M. F. (2017). Process-Driven Math: An auditory method of mathematics instruction and assessment for students who are blind or have low vision. *Journal of Visual Impairment & Blindness*, 111(5), 465–471. https://doi.org 10.1177/0145482X1711100507

Gulley, A.P. (2021). Examining Process-Driven Math: A user centered design and universal design for learning perspective. Doctoral dissertation, Auburn University. Auburn University Electronic Theses and Dissertations.

Halberstadt, A. G., Cooke, A. N., Garner, P. W., Hughes, S. A., Oertwig, D., & Neupert, S. D. (2020). Racialized emotion recognition accuracy and anger bias of children's faces. *Emotion.* https://doi.org/10.1037/emo0000756

Kendi, I.X. (2019). *How to be an antiracist.* Random House Publishing Group.

Kraemer J.D. & Benton C.S. (2015). Disparities in road crash mortality among pedestrians using wheelchairs in the USA: results of a capture–recapture analysis. *BMJ Open* 2015; 5:e008396. doi:10.1136/bmjopen-2015-008396

McReynolds, J.C. (2020). People [Recorded by J. McReynolds]. On People [EP].

Mohebbi, Behzad, The Art of Packaging: An investigation into the role of color in packaging, marketing, and branding (2014). *International Journal of Organizational Leadership* 3(2014), 92-102.

Pearson, Y.E., & Alexander, Q.G. (2020). Inclusion of persons with disabilities in STEM education and careers. Chapter 9, in *Implementation Strategies for Improving Diversity in Organizations*, IGI Global, Editor: C. Hughes.

Phillips, C. M. L., & Gulley, A. P., & Pearson, Y. E., & Prickett, L. C., & Smith, L. A., & Eyler, J., & Noble, S., & Ragland, M. F., & Price, J. A., & Shethia, A. K., & Perez, L., & Dunn, C. (2018, June). Solving problems of mathematics accessibility with Process-Driven Math: Methods and implications. Paper presented at 2018 ASEE Annual Conference & Exposition , Salt Lake City, Utah. 10.18260/1-2--30977

Sanders, K. Y. (2006). Overprotection and lowered expectations of persons with disabilities: The unforeseen consequences. *Work,* 27(2), 181-188.

Steele C. M. & Aronson J. (1995). Stereotype threat and the intellectual test performance of African Americans. *Journal of Personality and Social Psychology,* 69, 797-811.

Supermind Platforms. (2022). What causes anger? psychguides.com.

Vitug, E. ed. (2017). Dorothy J. Vaughan. In NACA and NASA Langley Hall of Honor Class of 2017. https://www.nasa.gov/langley/hall-of-honor/dorothy-j-vaughan

ACKNOWLEDGMENTS

I owe immeasurable debts of gratitude to everyone who encouraged me to write—and complete—this book and to each individual who has taken time to read it. Thank you.

I love and appreciate my aunts and uncles who are still with me—Myrtle Jefferson, Cleveland Jefferson, Cynthia Jackson Woods, Freddie Woods, Jr., Alfreda Jackson, and Sandra Jackson—as well as those who are not—Terry Jackson, Sr. and Donald Jackson—for all you taught me and everything you have poured into me throughout my entire life. Mom, thank you for everything.

None of this would have been possible without the support of a fantastic team of folks helping to pull it together. Alfreda Jackson and Geraldine Jackson—thank you for reading sample chapters early on and providing support and motivation for me to keep going. Helen Kalmans, Jacqueline Prince, and Alexandra Corinth—thank you for your editorial support and critiques along with marketing and design inputs and insights. Amber Weatherton, Logan Prickett, and Dr. Ann Gulley—thank you for allowing me to share your stories and helping me to articulate them. Dr. Nehemiah Mabry, thank you for your encouragement and support. Steve Kuhn—thank you for taking the time to get to know my work, my style, and my preferences to help you design a striking cover and interior.

Finally, thank you to everyone who has made a difference—positive or negative—in my life so I can share my lived experiences for the benefit of others.

ABOUT THE AUTHOR

Dr. Yvette E. Pearson is Vice President for Diversity, Equity and Inclusion at The University of Texas at Dallas and Founder and Principal Consultant of The PEER Group, LLC. Her university-based and consulting efforts have led to over $40 million in grant funding to support projects focused on the engagement and success of students from minoritized and marginalized identities. A Fellow of the American Society of Civil Engineers (ASCE), her work has led to changes in policies and practices to advance equity and inclusion in ASCE and other global organizations.

Dr. Pearson has been an invited speaker for events hosted by organizations such as the National Academy of Engineering, the UN Foundation, Brookings Institution, the American Association for the Advancement of Science, the World Federation of Engineering Organizations and numerous universities. She has been featured or quoted in media outlets such as Media Planet, Houston Chronicle, and Diverse: Issues in Higher Education.

A registered Professional Engineer, Dr. Pearson's awards and honors include ASCE's Professional Practice Ethics and Leadership Award, ABET's Claire L. Felbinger Award for Diversity and Inclusion, the Society of Women Engineers Distinguished Engineering Educator Award, and ASCE's President's Medal.

Her podcast, Engineering Change, has audiences in over 80 countries on six continents.